TOOLS FOR

Transition

IN **Early**

Childhood

TOOLS FOR

Transition

IN **Early**

Childhood

A Step-by-Step Guide
for Agencies,
Teachers, & Families

by

Beth S. Rous, Ed.D.
Interdisciplinary Human Development Institute
University of Kentucky
Lexington

and

Rena A. Hallam, Ph.D.
Department of Child and Family Studies
University of Tennessee
Knoxville

·P A U L·H·
BROOKES
PUBLISHING Co ®

Baltimore • London • Sydney

Paul H. Brookes Publishing Co.
Post Office Box 10624
Baltimore, Maryland 21285-0624

www.brookespublishing.com

Typeset by Graphic World, St. Louis, Missouri.
Manufactured in the United States of America by
Versa Press, Inc., East Peoria, Illinois.

The vignettes in this book are composites based on the authors' experiences. In most
instances, names and identifying details have been changed to protect confidentiality. In
all other cases, individuals' names and stories are used by permission.

Tools for Transition in Early Childhood was based in part on work conducted through Grant Nos.
G008401551, O24D90023, H024D90023, and H024D60011 from the U.S. Department of
Education (USDOE), Office of Special Education Programs. However, the opinions expressed do
not necessarily reflect the position or policy of USDOE, and no official endorsement by the
Department of Education should be inferred.

Library of Congress Cataloging-in-Publication Data

Rous, Beth S.
  Tools for transition in early childhood: a step-by-step guide for agencies, teachers, and
  families / by Beth S. Rous and Rena A. Hallam.
    p.   cm.
  Includes bibliographical references and index.
  ISBN-13: 978-1-55766-735-9
  ISBN-10: 1-55766-735-7
  1. Child care services-United States.   2. Child care services—Government policy—
  United States.   3. Early childhood education—United States.   4. Children with disabilities—
  Services for—United States.   5. Children with disabilities—Education-United States.
  I. Hallam, Rena A.   II. Title.

  HQ778.63.R68 2006
  362.71'2—dc22   2006028233

British Library Cataloguing in Publication data are available from the British Library.

Contents

About the Authors

Beth S. Rous, Ed.D., is the Director for Early Childhood and Community Education at the Interdisciplinary Human Development Institute, University of Kentucky, Lexington. She began her career as a teacher, where she worked in public and private child care and taught at the preschool, elementary, and middle-school levels. Her research has involved a variety of topics in early childhood education and early childhood special education, including transition, standards and accountability, professional development systems, and program quality. She has published numerous articles, technical and training manuals, and book chapters. For almost 20 years, Dr. Rous provided training and technical assistance through a number of federally funded demonstration, outreach, and research projects, most notably the Sequenced Transition to Education in the Public Schools (STEPS) program, on which much of this book is based. She has served in leadership roles in multiple professional organizations, most recently as President of the Division for Early Childhood of the Council for Exceptional Children.

Rena A. Hallam, Ph.D., is the Executive Director of the Early Learning Center for Research and Practice and Assistant Professor in the Department of Child and Family Studies, University of Tennessee, Knoxville. She has served in an administrative capacity in both child care and Head Start settings. Her research interests focus on systemic issues related to the quality of early care and education programs with a particular focus on children living in poverty. Specifically, she has studied transition, assessment and accountability, personnel preparation in early education, and state initiatives to improve child care quality. Dr. Hallam also has served as a STEPS trainer and has collaborated with many local communities to devise, implement, and evaluate local interagency efforts to improve transition practices.

Foreword

Transitions between important events are repeated occurrences in the life cycle of humans in western society (Bailey, 1988). Those transitions often are influenced and imposed by cultural and societal practices. Many transitions are recognized by most members of society, are predictable, and have societal supports and expectations. For example, in the United States, transitioning to formal public schooling often occurs at age 5. Families and children alike anticipate public schooling with a mixture of excitement and dread. Schools prepare for it, and extended family members regard it as a significant event in children's lives. Although such transitions sometimes are associated with stress or anxiety, they also are viewed as adaptive and normative.

When a child is born with a disability or when a disability is recognized during the early years, children and families come in contact with service providers of various sorts. These contacts with professionals and the services and activities they provide are not normative, although they are often welcomed. What families do not anticipate but invariably experience is transitions in those services (Rosenkoetter, Whaley, Hains, & Pierce, 2001). These transitions take many different forms, such as from one home visitor or therapist to others. Other transitions are more bewildering, such as the transition from Part C services to preschool services under the public schools. Families shift from one agency with a set of rules, regulations, service providers, expectations, and supports to another agency with different rules, regulations, service providers, expectations, and supports. Of course, soon after the Part C transitions, families encounter a transition to school-age services, which startlingly often has even different rules and expectations. Families sometimes report shifts from a system in which they felt supported and helped to systems whose expectations are for the family to help the professionals accomplish their (the professionals') goals with the child—a shift from, "We are here to help you" to "Here's what you need to do so your child will learn better in school," a shift from "How are things going?" to "What are you going to do about your child's problem behavior at school?"

Is it any wonder when families are surprised by a transition, are fearful of the outcomes, appear concerned about what the transition will mean for their child, or are stressed by it? Is it any wonder that these transitions seem illogical to families? When children are identified early, families may encounter professionals whom the family considers helpful and supportive, and ideally strong positive relationships emerge. In such cases, families may perceive no pressing need to mess with a good thing; a transition may imply a loss of contact with a caring professional. When children are identified later (e.g., as with young children with autism), the transition may occur quickly after a child is diagnosed and has started receiving services. Families of such children are surprised by the transition, because they are just getting started.

As professionals, we understand why those transitions exist from Part C to preschool services and from preschool services to school-age services. Some of us can remember when no assistance or services were available to families of young children with developmental delays and disabilities. Before the Education of the Handicapped Act Amendments of 1986 (PL 99-457), the transition was often from nothing to something for school-age children. Nonetheless, transitions exist in our service system, and we have a responsibility to help families and children make those transitions with minimal disruption to the family and for the benefit of the child. This book addresses these transitions and how we as professionals can help families through those transitions. It is primarily about how we can help our various service systems change so that the transitions are less disruptive and are more adaptive—indeed more normative.

Beth Rous, lead author of this book, is no newcomer to transitions. In the late 1980s, she assumed the directorship of a Handicapped Children's Early Education Program project titled, Sequenced Transitions into Education in the Public Schools (STEPS; Rous, Hemmeter, & Schuster, 1994). Based on the work of earlier colleagues (e.g., Rita Byrd and Peggy Stephens) in that project, she expanded the effort and began statewide training efforts focused on systems change to promote better transitions. She has continued this interest in and exploration of issues related to transitions through the work of the National Early Childhood Transition Center at the University of Kentucky with her co-author on this book, Rena Hallam.

In this book, Rous and Hallam describe a community-based approach for establishing transition processes and policies. Thus, the approach is inherently ecological and involves interagency collaboration. A process model for transitions planning, execution, and evaluation are presented in Chapter 1. In subsequent chapters, the authors elaborate on specific elements of the model.

Rather than providing a chapter-by-chapter description in this foreword, five themes appearing across chapters are noted. First, in keeping with the interagency focus, this book is for professionals working with children who have and do not have disabilities. The explicit assumption is that all programs and agencies working with young children have a stake in, potentially encounter problems with, and can contribute to the solutions related to the transitions their children and families face. As such, this is not a disability-specific book, yet it holds tremendous potential for improving services to young children with disabilities.

Second, the model, its elements, and the suggested steps and practices are based on the professional literature and on experience. The research literature on transitions is relatively sparse and spread over 2 or 3 decades, but the authors draw on related literatures when appropriate (e.g., on team functioning). However, the content of this book is enriched by the knowledge and experience of the authors working to help various communities improve their transition practices for young children. Thus, readers will find real-world questions and issues in these pages. More important, however, the reader will find relevant suggestions and wise guidance grounded in years of addressing these issues.

Third, the manner in which information is presented and the content of this book are highly practical. This practicality in presentation is seen in the reader-friendly prose, the permission to photocopy relevant forms, the useful figures and tables, and the two case examples used across chapters. Evidence of the practicality of the content is seen in discussions as important but is easily overlooked regarding whether interagency team members have the authority from their home agencies to contribute meaningfully in planning and revising community-wide transition practices. Similarly, the authors suggest practices that can be used for identifying and addressing idiosyncratic community problems (barriers) to transitions. Furthermore, the suggested practices are highly transportable across agencies and across communities.

Fourth, many elements of the transition process model are presented in substantial detail—relevant issues are not glossed over. For example, the authors present highly useful and detailed information on holding interagency team meetings, making decisions by such teams, and so forth. This information, if heeded, will save such groups substantial time, build cohesion across members, and reduce misunderstandings. This book is about the nuts and bolts of engaging in communitywide efforts to improve the transitions for young children. It is not a cookbook; it is about a complex social process whereby different stakeholders join together to make their community a better place for children and families.

Finally, this book—despite its detail and practicality—is about a flexible process. No one-size-fits-all approach is advocated. The process of interagency building and working is presented in the context of transitions for young children. However, the steps, suggestions, and practices are relevant to other issues such as Child Find and early identification, building multiple placement options in a community for young children with disabilities, and other resource and service allocation issues. In fact, much of this book would be relevant to creating better transitions from school to work for youth with disabilities. Let me be clear. This book is about early childhood transitions, and readers interested in this issue will find much meat for thought and for practice. The processes, principles, and practices, however, are about interagency work—regardless of the focus of the work.

In summary, Rous and Hallam give the field a very sound, practical, detailed, and flexible approach to early childhood transitions for children with and without disabilities and their families. This statement should not be taken to mean they present an easy approach—interagency work by its very nature is rarely easy. It calls on each of us to behave without self-interest and in rational ways. If 5 or 10 years hence, early childhood transitions across the communities of this nation are no more logical, no smoother for families, no more facilitative than they are now, then it will not be the fault of Rous and Hallam. They have given us a small book full of big ideas requiring hard but necessary work. If the model is applied, then the lives of many young children and families will be spared unnecessary stress, worry, discomfort, and uncertainty, and educational resources will be conserved. These outcomes would be a significant contribution.

Mark Wolery, Ph.D.
Professor of Special Education
Peabody College, Vanderbilt University

REFERENCES

Bailey, D.B. (1988). Assessing critical events. In D.B. Bailey & R.J. Simeonsson (Eds.) *Family assessment in early intervention* (pp. 119–138). Columbus, OH: Merrill.

Education of the Handicapped Act Amendments of 1986, PL 99-457, 20 U.S.C. §§ 1400 *et seq.*

Rosenkoetter, S.E., Whaley, K.T., Hains, A.H., & Pierce, L. (2001). The evolution of transition policy for young children with special needs and their families: Past, present, and future. *Topics in Early Childhood Special Education, 21,* 3–15.

Rous, B., Hemmeter, M.L., & Schuster, J.S. (1994). Sequenced transition to education in the public schools: A systems approach to transition planning. *Topics in Early Childhood Special Education, 14,* 374–393.

Acknowledgments

The writing of this book would not have been possible without the hard work and dedication of the many states and communities that have participated in training and outreach through the Sequenced Transition to Education in the Public Schools (STEPS) program. This includes the state and local transition teams from Alaska, Delaware, Florida, Georgia, Hawaii, Indiana, Kentucky, Missouri, North Carolina, Ohio, Tennessee, South Carolina, Texas, and Washington. These teams did the hard work of making transition meaningful to children, families, and staff. We were constantly amazed at the creativity by which they approached challenges and promoted positive change.

At another level, the STEPS facilitators across the country provided countless hours of discussion, problem solving, and support to us and to the local transition teams, most especially Susan Duwa (FL), Mike Fahey (HI), Bobbi Figdor (AK), Harriet Foiles (MO), Bettianne Ford (FL), Mary Janson (OH), Jim Lesko (DE), Katherine McCormick (GA and KY), Germaine O'Connell (KY), Mary Jo Paladino (IN), Gene Perotta (NC), Ann Shureen Smith (WA), Polly Taylor (ID), Amy Valdez (HI), and Lynn Yamashita (HI). A special note of thanks goes to Brenda Mullins who has worked tirelessly to make transitions work in Kentucky and who helped create some of the figures and tables in Chapters 7 and 8. She is a phenomenal trainer, facilitator, and overall motivator to all who know and work with her.

A note of thanks also to our colleagues from the National Early Childhood Transition Research and Training Center who have spent numerous hours thinking about transition and ways to promote more successful transitions for children and families across the country. This includes our research partners, Ann Hains, Gloria Harbin, Mark Innocenti, Katherine McCormick, Teri Nowak, Sharon Rosenkoetter, and Sarintha Stricklin, and our research staff, Emily Keely, Minda Kohner-Coogle, Colleen McClanahan, Carol Schroeder, Jordan Shaw, Christine Teeters, and Patrick Yacobi.

Finally, the work represented in this book would not have been possible without the foresight and creativity of a wonderful group of early childhood professionals in Kentucky. This group started the process of thinking about transition in the early 1980s, wrote a federal grant, and started a legacy. Thank you to the leadership provided by Peggy Stephens Hayden and Dr. Mark Wolery; the tireless efforts of Rita Byrd, Linda Dyk, and Ellen Perry; and the staff at Cardinal Hill Preschool, Child Development Centers, Growing Together, and Fayette County Public Schools at the time that this work was being done. We owe them a debt of gratitude.

Chapter 1

A Community Approach to Transition

Since the 1980s, a dramatic shift has taken place in the status of early care and education programs. This shift has occurred for a number of reasons. First, an unparalleled increase in the number of young children and families participating in early care and education programs has been a result of the growing needs of single-parent families and families in which both parents work outside the home (Children's Defense Fund, 2003). In 1999, more than 10.5 million children were being cared for by caregivers other than their parents while their parents worked (U.S. Census Bureau, 2004). According to this census data, while 38% of young children in America receive care solely from their parents, 62% receive care from a variety of caregivers including relatives, non-relatives, and center-based programs. The quality of these early care and education programs and the experiences of young children within these environments are critically important.

The second reason for the shift in status of early care and education programs is the passage of the Education of the Handicapped Act (EHA) Amendments of 1986 (PL 99-457) and its subsequent amendments. Because of these amendments, families and their young children have increased access to early intervention and preschool special education programs. The 2004

Office of Special Education Programs *Report to Congress* (U.S. Department of Education, 2004) reported that 267,923 infants and toddlers and 647,000 3- to 5-year-olds received services through these programs. As represented by the reauthorization of the EHA and the subsequent reauthorizations of the Individuals with Disabilities Education Act (IDEA) of 1990 (PL 101-476), Congress continually has recognized the complexities inherent in the lives of young children with disabilities and their families and has mandated transition planning as a part of the services provided for these young children and their families. These mandates include services and supports that are designed to help families of children with disabilities navigate a complex system that involves multiple disciplines and diverse funding sources and program approaches. These supports and services are designed to support families as they move among the various agencies that provide services.

The federal law provided the impetus and administrative infrastructure to implement needed services. This infrastructure includes a division in the administration of the federal program across two age ranges: birth to age 3 (infants and toddlers) and 3- to 4-year-olds (preschoolers). The preschool program is housed within state departments of education; however, states may choose a lead agency for the infant and toddler program and are given flexibility in the design of the service delivery models used across programs. This has resulted in great variability between the early intervention and preschool service delivery systems not only across states but also often within states as well (Harbin, McWilliam, & Gallagher, 2000).

The third reason for the shift in status of early care and education programs is that both state and federal governments have increased the number of publicly funded programs for children who are considered at risk in an effort to better prepare all children to succeed in school. Examples include the expansion of the Head Start program, the establishment of Early Head Start (U.S. Department of Health & Human Services, 2001, 2002), and the increase of public prekindergarten programs across the country (Blank, Schulman, & Ewen, 1999). According to the National Institute for Early Education Research (NIEER), 38 states served nearly 740,000 children through their state prekindergarten initiatives alone (Barnett, Hustedt, Robin, & Schulman, 2004).

This increase in publicly funded programs has provided expanded opportunities for young children and their families; however, many of the programs do not operate full-day, full-year programs. For example, some programs offer half-day programs, some operate on a school schedule, and some have a shortened week schedule (e.g., 4 days per week). Families who are part of the workforce often must piece together a full day of care for their children by using multiple programs across a day, week, or year. This can contribute to greater movement between and among agencies for children and families, requiring greater levels of transition planning and collaboration across agencies and programs.

Although many policy and demographic factors have converged to influence the transitions experienced by young children and their families, the complexity, divergence, and episodic nature of the early care and education system in the United States necessitates quality transition planning. As the field of early care and education has responded to the increasing need for early childhood services at both the state and federal level, programs have been developed across numerous agencies for a variety of purposes. Such programs include child care services, Title I, the aforementioned Head Start, early intervention, Even Start, and public preschool, all of which are housed and administered through separate organizations and initiatives (Harbin, Rous, & McLean, 2005). As a result, the funding streams, regulatory requirements, administration, program guidelines, and even research foci have often been disparate and sometimes even contradictory. This lack of continuity among programs, coupled with an absence of systems designed to support and facilitate the transition process, often make the transition for children and families difficult (Love, Logue, Trudeau, & Thayer, 1992).

TRANSITION OVERVIEW

Transition involves a process of movement or change from one environment to another. This movement or change in programs or services brings new opportunities and challenges for staff, families, and children. These transitions have been described as occurring both horizontally and vertically (Kagan, 1992). Horizontal transitions involve movement or change in services within a common timeframe. For example, Johnny may go from home to Head Start and then to the child care program over the course of 1 day. Vertical transitions involve movement or change across time. For example, Johnny may leave the early intervention program and move to the public school preschool program at age 3. Within both horizontal and vertical transitions, young children and their families can experience a variety of changes.

Some transitions involve a shift or change in the program that provides overall services to the child and/or the family. For example, after birth, children leave the hospital setting to go home. Once home, many children make the transition to child care, a family child care home, or another structured program so that their parents can work. At the age of 3, infants and toddlers with disabilities move from early intervention services to public preschool programs, Head Start, a child care program, or home. When children reach school age, they may make a transition from the preschool program, child care, or Head Start to kindergarten or first grade.

Another type of transition involves changes in the curriculum or structure of the program or classroom. For example, a teacher in an Early Head Start program may use the Creative Curriculum (Dodge, Colker, Heroman, & Bickart, 2002). Another teacher working with the child may use a Montessori or High/Scope approach. In addition to changes in curriculum, changes in the theoretical or philosophical approach of the program or classroom may occur.

One program may follow a traditional constructivist approach whereas another may be inspired by the programs of Reggio Emilia. Finally, transition can also involve changes in the providers, teachers, and staff with whom both children and families interact.

DEVELOPING A COMMUNITYWIDE TRANSITION SYSTEM

To help address these multiple transitions in the lives of young children and families, a systematic process for ensuring that children and families move successfully among these various agencies and programs needs to be established. This involves developing collaborative relationships with other agencies in the community, negotiating key issues and procedures, and formalizing agreements. When agencies and programs collaborate, they must make decisions together about the activities, policies, and procedures they will be using to address transition. Therefore, transition involves an *interagency system that assesses the transition concerns of the whole community while ensuring through interagency policies and procedure the successful movement of children and families among agencies.*

Every agency that serves young children has faced issues related to the movement of a child and family from a current program to a new agency. In many cases, agencies and programs have addressed transition as a series of events that prepare children and families. In this book, we propose thinking about transition in the context of a community system. This system involves community agencies and schools working together to develop a vision for transition and to plan transition services that are congruent across service providers within the community.

The strategies and tools that are provided in this book are based on a number of guiding principles that can guide a community transition system development approach.

1. *Communities must develop a consistent transition vision that can be used to drive decisions related to transition practices and activities.* The vision that is used by the team must be developed with input from all of the key stakeholders in the community. From that point on, the vision serves as the major decision broker, meaning that all decisions are based on whether the resulting action moves the team closer to the vision.

2. *The transition system must be built so that it integrates with existing structures and systems.* Transition planning is not a stand-alone event. It is a complex activity often supported by other program services and features. For example, transition planning related to preparing children for new environments is difficult to separate from the general curriculum in the classroom. Therefore, transition activities must be considered in the context of these other services.

3. *Keep it simple: Use a system that is comprehensive and effective but not unnecessarily elaborate.* This old adage is certainly true where transition is concerned. In determining the best way to address transition issues, the simplest approach is most often the most successful. Elaborate systems tend to be hard to implement and maintain.

4. *Understand that resolving "old" concerns and problems may create new ones.* As is true with most systems change efforts, the efforts that fix or address one issue commonly have an impact on another part of the system. For example, the transition team may determine that they need a common referral form that can be used across agencies. The result may be a need for changes in agency policies and procedures to include the new forms and new training for staff on the use of the forms and procedures.

Several key issues need to be kept in mind as communities begin the process of addressing transition in a systemic way. First, *stakeholder involvement is critical* to successful systems development. This includes families and all agency or program staff that participate in and support the transition process, from administrators to teachers to related services personnel (e.g., therapists, psychologists). Second, interagency collaboration is an essential part of the transition systems development process. Therefore, as stakeholders begin the task of determining key issues and barriers to successful transitions and determining the most appropriate strategies and activities to implement on a community level, they should include specific strategies that *promote and support interagency collaboration.* Third, developing transition processes that are congruent across agencies and programs requires *time and commitment* on the part of everyone involved. As agencies embark on this adventure, they should remember that stakeholders will not always agree about the best approach to take. In fact, *agreement is an outcome of true collaboration,* not vice versa. The more collaborative agencies become, the more they will begin to agree about important issues. Fourth and finally, the team needs to remember the various approaches to transition systems design work. *There is no one right way.* The important goal is for key stakeholders to develop a system that meets their specific concerns and takes into consideration their community and program attributes.

THE ROLE OF COLLABORATION

Collaboration among agencies and programs is critical when developing communitywide transition systems; the key lies in understanding what collaboration is and is not. Collaboration is not about always agreeing to the actions or suggestions of others. Collaboration is about valuing the opinions and viewpoints of other stakeholders, sharing responsibility for the actions of the team, and contributing equally to the work. In beginning the process of collaboration, agencies and programs can think of the continuum of relationships that one program or agency can have with other agencies in the community. The continuum in Figure 1.1 represents four stages in the relationship between agencies: communication, cooperation, coordination, and collaboration. The overall goal is to support the community's ability to design high-quality transition systems, which indicates that collaborative relationships have been built, with all key stakeholders participating on the transition team. Collaboration is hard work and takes much time and effort on the part of all team members.

Assessing the Status of Community Relationships in Transition

Throughout the last month, Mary has been busy developing relationships with other early childhood agencies in the Hobart community. She met with John to discuss the transition team and their activities. She also was able to provide information to the local child care program about services offered in the public school for their spring parent meeting. Last week, the local early intervention program contacted her about participating in a Child Find fair that they were planning. She has agreed to send some of her staff to the event to help register parents for school.

● ● ●

In the communication continuum, the further along the continuum one goes, the more time one must invest in the relationship; the more time invested in the relationship, the more successful the outcome for families and children. Within this continuum, the following definitions can be helpful in assessing community relationships across agencies.

Communication is the exchange of information between individuals or groups of individuals. Communication can be in the form of a conversation

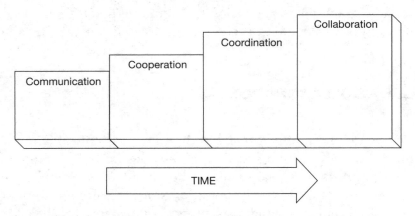

Figure 1.1. Stages of relationships in transition system development.

that occurs between two individuals or a response to a request from another agency or individual. For example, in the previous vignette, Mary is communicating (exchanging information) with John in the Head Start program about the transition plan that the community has in place.

Cooperation is evidenced by the willingness of an agency or individual to comply with the request of another agency or individual. Cooperation can be seen as helping or assisting another in his or her pursuit of an action, activity, or goal. Mary cooperated (assisted or complied) with the child care program by sending information to them so that they could have it for their parent meeting.

Coordination is the bringing together of resources for a common purpose. When agencies coordinate their activities, one agency determines the desired activity or action and other agencies agree to support the action and match resources (e.g., money, staff time, materials). Mary was coordinating with the local early intervention program when she agreed that her agency would participate in and provide resources for their Child Find event.

Collaboration is the final level on the continuum. In a collaborative arrangement, programs join forces and pool resources to accomplish a commonly identified goal. For Mary, collaboration would be evident if she and the other agencies on the transition team had identified a joint Child Find effort as a need, worked together to plan the event, and then pooled resources and worked in partnership to implement the activity.

Agencies may be at different points along the continuum on different activities and in their relationships with different agencies. For example, the early intervention program may communicate with the Head Start Program, coordinate with the local health department, and collaborate with the local school system. The Determining Community Relationships form in Figure 1.2—in this case completed for Mary from the previous vignette—can help agencies identify where along the continuum they are with respect to specific transition activities or events. A blank, photocopiable Determining Community Relationships form appears on page 166 in the appendix.

ORGANIZATION OF THIS BOOK

This book focuses on providing information, resources, and tools for implementing a transition model that recognizes transition planning as a community process and provides a framework that supports collaborative planning activities across agencies and programs. A series of well-defined steps and strategies are outlined to help move a community along a continuum of transition systems design. These steps are designed to take into consideration the interagency nature of transition as well as the contextual variables that will influence the success of the transition process as measured by positive child outcomes. The remainder of this book provides a detailed overview of each of the steps, as presented in Figure 1.3.

Determining Community Relationships

Major stakeholder agencies	Transition-related activities	Current relationship			
		Communicate (exchange, respond)	Cooperate (comply, help)	Coordinate (organize, match)	Collaborate (join forces, pool)
Hobart Public Schools	Spring registration			X	
	Child Find		X		
ABC Child Care	School visitation program				X
Hobart Early Intervention Program	Referral and intake	X			
	Child Find		X		
Hobart Health Department	Vision and hearing screening			X	

Figure 1.2. Determining community relationships. Sample: Hobart County, USA.

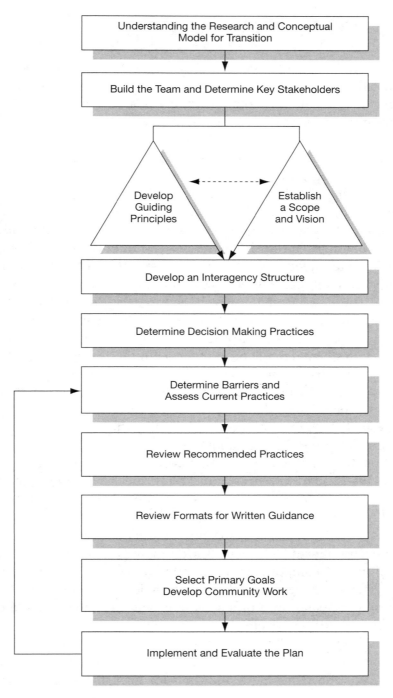

Figure 1.3. Overview of the transition process.

To help support the community team in implementing the recommendations provided in this book, two case studies are used throughout the text that represent two different communities: Hobart County and Metroville. These communities are described in detail in Chapter 3.

Chapter 2 provides an overview of transition research. It introduces a conceptual model for a systematic process for the transition of young children from one environment, program, or service to another.

Chapter 3 provides information on how to set up a transition team that represents the key stakeholders in the community. Information and recommendations for identifying key stakeholders—agencies with which young children and families in transition are most commonly involved—in the transition process are provided. This chapter also asks the reader to consider how young children and families will be involved in the transition system design and operation. These determinations will lead to decisions related to the interagency planning and administrative structures (which will likely be refined as planning progresses). Finally, a process for creating a shared vision is presented. This includes a systematic process for defining the big picture through characteristics of the transition system that the team wants to establish related to the varied audiences whom the system will serve (e.g., young children, families, teachers, vocational rehabilitation therapists, other agency representatives). Once established, this vision should become the cornerstone for decision making across all aspects of transition.

Chapter 4 helps the team define the interagency structure that will be used to plan and oversee transition. Two critical components of the interagency structure are addressed: 1) operation and participation and 2) meeting structure. Emphasis is placed on active involvement of all participants so that transition is not seen as the responsibility of only one agency. Specific information about each topic and worksheets are provided to record team decisions about each of the key components. This section is designed to support a system of ongoing interagency structure that will be able to respond effectively to the various changes, issues, and problems that will inevitably emerge over time that affect the transition system.

Chapter 5 provides information and tools to help the team determine how decisions will be made on a collaborative basis. The basic types of decisions are introduced, and worksheets and tools for formalizing team decisions are provided.

Chapter 6 provides a process for determining current barriers to effective transitions in the community. Tools for assessing the current status of communication across agencies and the status of standard transition practices both within individual agencies and on a community basis are provided. This chapter is intended to help the reader build on existing structures, policies, and procedures rather than replacing them or establishing a separate system for transition.

Chapter 7 provides information on a variety of administrative and staff practices that have been recommended in the literature as supporting transition planning. These include assuming responsibility for the transition process, developing transition procedures, facilitating communication among agency staff, maintaining staff and family involvement in the transition process, providing professional development opportunities, enhancing staff communication across agencies, facilitating staff involvement in determining transition policies and procedures, and encouraging staff involvement in preparing children for transition.

Chapter 8 provides information on practices that have been recommended in the literature for enhancing family involvement in transition planning and for supporting child preparation for and adjustment to new environments. These practices include ensuring awareness of program options, providing information and determining strategies for addressing family and child concerns, understanding and identifying entry-level skills, and providing individual transition planning.

Chapter 9 provides information on the variety of ways that agencies can support transition activities through written guidance. This written guidance includes policies, procedures, interagency agreements, and technical guidance developed on an intra- and interagency basis.

Chapter 10 provides tips and tools for determining priority areas and for developing an annual work plan and action steps for addressing issues identified and for implementing key activities identified by the transition team.

Chapter 11 provides suggestions and strategies for how to evaluate a new transition system so that annual improvements can be made.

The purpose of this book is to help programs coordinate their services and plan transitions that ensure young children's school readiness. The remainder of this book provides the transition team with detailed information on how to develop a communitywide transition process and includes case examples and question-and-answer sections in each chapter to help make the strategies easy to implement. To better assist the team, photocopiable forms are provided in the appendix for the phases of the planning process.

Facilitating effective and supportive transitions for young children and families requires thoughtful and deliberate planning at the community and agency level. This book provides a framework for thinking and planning that is systematic, useful, and flexible so that unique local needs can be addressed and considered in the transition planning process.

Chapter 2

Research Base

with Gloria Harbin, Katherine McCormick,
and Lee Ann Jung

The study of transition experiences of young children and their families is a complicated endeavor. The multidimensional nature of transition requires seeking to understand relationships and processes across agencies, staff, families, and children in a specific community context. Transition research in the field of early care and education has attempted to examine issues relevant to the experiences of children and families, professional development, and interagency structure at the state and local levels. This chapter synthesizes the current transition research in the field of early care and education and outlines a conceptual framework for the transition planning process described in this book. This process focuses on vertical transitions—transitions that involve movement or change across time—that occur at often predictable points for young children and their families, specifically the transition experiences from home to some type of group care and from preschool to kindergarten.

As mentioned in Chapter 1, moving from program to program and from provider to provider requires adjustments for both the child and family. Program models, philosophy, and staffing patterns often vary significantly across agencies serving infants and toddlers, preschoolers, and kindergartners. As transition points are encountered, all families may have concerns about

Gloria Harbin, Ph.D., is Senior Research Scientist, FPG Child Development Institute, The University of North Carolina at Chapel Hill; Katherine McCormick, Ph.D., is Associate Professor, Department of Special Education and Rehabilitation Sciences, University of Kentucky; Lee Ann Jung, Ph.D., is Assistant Professor, Department of Special Education and Rehabilitation Sciences, University of Kentucky.

finding appropriate services, maintaining continuity of services, and meeting the changing concerns of their child and family (Hanline, 1988). However, the stress felt at transition periods can be exacerbated for families of young children with disabilities (Fowler, Chandler, Johnson, & Stella, 1988; Karr-Jelinek, 1994).

The literature in early childhood transition contains evidence of the organizational complexities and the resulting problems experienced by families, children, and the professionals who provide services. For example, Entwisle and Alexander (1998) found that a child's preschool experience and initial transition to school had a direct impact on the child's later success, both academically and socially in a high-risk population. Children who experience poor transitions may be more vulnerable to mental health and adjustment problems, have less academic success, and have more difficulty with social relationships with their peers. These results are potentially compounded when children have been diagnosed with disabilities and need special services. In addition, research has documented that the implementation of specific transition practices at kindergarten entry can result in positive academic outcomes for children (Schulting, Malone, & Dodge, 2005).

Research on transition has provided valuable information about the individual variables that affect the transition process for children, families, and professionals. Much of this research has focused on the transition of children (with and without disabilities) among agencies. In response to the increase in the number and types of early childhood programs and the fragmentation of the early childhood system, much of the research on transition has shifted to a more ecological perspective underscoring the inherent complexity in understanding and affecting the early care and education context in the United States (Pianta & Cox, 1999; Ramey & Ramey, 1998).

Although transitions are unique experiences for all young children and families, research has demonstrated that children and families often confront challenges during times of transition between early childhood programs. For children with disabilities, several distinguishing characteristics can create challenges in transition planning and processes. For example, the transition process for young children with disabilities is more regulated than the transition process for typically developing children participating in early childhood programs. Specific regulations are provided regarding when and how transition planning should occur. This includes specific expectations related to data collection and documentation of transition experiences by local providers and state agencies. In addition, young children with disabilities, specifically those with significant disabilities, often have limited access to high-quality inclusive early childhood programs. Therefore, transition planning must take into consideration not only what needs to happen to prepare the child and family for the transition process but also whether the environments to which the child will make the transition are appropriate.

A CONCEPTUAL MODEL FOR TRANSITION

In an effort to be sensitive to the concerns of children with and without disabilities and their families, Rous, Hallam, Harbin, and McCormick have developed a framework for conceptualizing the transition planning process. Initially, this model was developed to address the concerns of children with disabilities only; however, the primary components of the model provide a means to thoughtfully consider and plan for effective transitions for all children with and without disabilities across many types of early care and education programs. The proposed conceptual model is based on the research literature, a systemic ecological orientation, and prior theoretical work on transition. The conceptual model is proposed to describe how the complex interactions of multiple systems interact to influence the transition process. In addition, the model delineates key interagency variables that are posited to affect the preparation and adjustment of young children and their families as they move among programs.

The transition model is depicted at two distinct levels. The first level, illustrated in Figure 2.1, reflects the traditional ecological model (Bronfenbrenner, 1986). It delineates specific elements in the ecological context that are proposed to particularly influence the transition experiences of young children and their families, in particular factors related to teachers and other early childhood care providers, early care and education programs, local community systems, and state systems. This depiction allows for a broader understanding of the multidimensional factors that influence the transition experiences of young children and families.

The second level of the model, shown in Figure 2.2, illustrates the specific program and community factors that most heavily influence the transition process and the immediate outcomes of child and family preparation and adjustment. A more detailed description of each of the major components of the model is presented next.

Ecological Contextual Factors

The proposed model provides a means to begin to understand the interplay between child and family factors with agency and community factors specifically as these factors relate to the transition process. The following section describes some of the key aspects of the ecological framework in relationship to the transition process.

Child Factors   The child is at the center of the transition process during the early childhood years. Characteristics of the child are critical to a high-quality transition process at the individual child level as well as at the community

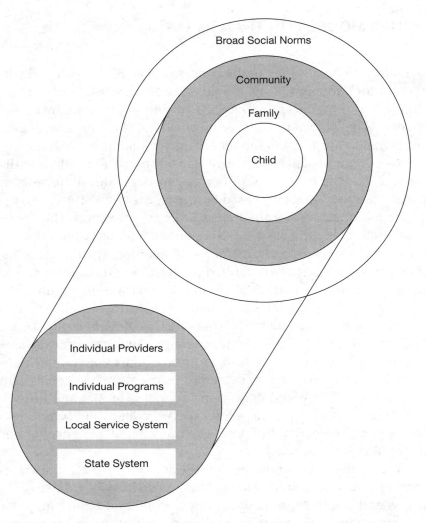

Figure 2.1. Traditional ecological model of transition.

systems level. The bioecological model highlights the importance of genetic factors, as well as environmental factors, in understanding the trajectory of a child's development (Bronfenbrenner & Morris, 1998). These individual child factors should inform the transition practices of all children (Pianta, Rimm-Kaufman, & Cox, 1999). In the case of children with disabilities, distinctive characteristics of the child that need to be considered for transition include nature and type of disability as well as child age. Individualized planning for young children with disabilities is a central element of supporting effective transition practices (Rosenkoetter, Whaley, Hains, & Pierce, 2001). In the complex case of transition, specifically, the child's date of birth has a direct impact on when the transition process occurs. For example, federal regulations that guide implementation of early intervention services mandate that children must transition out of early intervention at age 3, unless the state has developed specific policies to

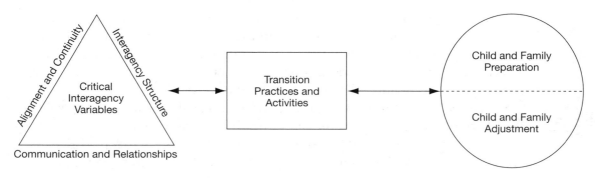

Figure 2.2. Specific program and community factors of transition model.

allow the child to remain in early intervention services (Individuals with Disabilities Education Improvement Act [IDEA] of 2004, PL 108-446).

Family Factors Families who participate in childhood education services represent a diverse population. This diversity includes several dimensions that influence a family's ability to participate in and receive support during the transition process. Professionals who facilitate the transition process must consider the resources and concerns of families and recognize that transitions do not occur in isolation from the social supports on which families typically rely (Hanline, 1993). Family culture, income and resources, and the family composition (e.g., foster families, single parents) influence the ways in which families make decisions and significantly enhance or diminish families' participation in the educational system (Moles, 1993). In addition, families hold different expectations and attitudes about early childhood programs and transition to kindergarten specifically (Diamond, Reagan, & Bandyk, 2000). Other factors that may affect the transition process include a family's experiences such as parenting experiences and previous as well as current experiences with the education system (Hoover-Dempsey & Sandler, 1997). These experiences can influence the expectations that the family has for their child as well as the nature of their involvement and their interactions with the child. Other factors that families bring to the transition process include family concerns and priorities, knowledge of rights and service options, ability to advocate, support from family and friends, and the ability to adapt to change.

Community Factors From an ecological perspective, children, families, and service providers are directly supported, both economically and socially, by the communities in which they live. Within this context are several broader community factors that potentially can affect the transition services available to families and children (Harbin, McWilliam, & Gallagher, 2000; Shonkoff & Phillips, 2000). The resources available for early childhood programs can be directly influenced by the economic status of the community (Edwards, 1980;

Van Horn & Van Meter, 1977), the political will within the community (Harbin, McWilliam, et al., 1998; Van Horn & Van Meter, 1977), and the value the community places on the development of young children (Harbin et al., 2000). Additional demographic factors, such as geographic status (e.g., urban, rural), crime rate, and the job market also should be considered.

Within the community are four specific levels of variables that specifically influence the transition process for young children and families: provider, program, service system, and state. *Provider factors* refers to the providers who work directly with the child and family and who have a great deal of responsibility for facilitating the transition process. Because professionals in early childhood programs have a wide range of educational backgrounds and represent many disciplines (e.g., physical therapy, occupational therapy, early childhood special education), the education, training, and experience of these providers, including their professional discipline, must be considered as potential contributing factors to the nature and success of the transition process (Rosenkoetter, Hains, & Fowler, 1994). Another important factor is a provider's knowledge of the skills needed by the child in the next environment. Additional training related to transition can play a role in the provider's ability to support the transition process and can help shape his or her overall philosophy for service delivery and transition planning (Conn-Powers, Ross-Allen, & Holburn, 1990). Personal characteristics such as interpersonal skills, ability to work well with adults and children, and temperament must be considered, given the key role of communication and the importance of relationships in the transition process.

Individual program factors refer to the diverse and divergent programs that serve young children, which combine with the importance of continuity in transition planning to make the overall design of programs a consideration in transition planning, specifically related to quality and overall philosophy. The transition process is greatly influenced by the community of learners and climate for learning (Dunst, Hamby, Trivette, Raab, & Bruder, 2000). This includes attention to not only specific instructional techniques used to facilitate learning but also the environments in which these services are offered. The administrative structure of the program also plays a key role in the transition process, specifically the support and philosophy of the leadership and management, the program policies and procedures, and the funding structure as it relates to supporting staff in their participation in quality transition practices (Harbin & Salisbury, 2000; Salisbury, Palombaro, & Hollowood, 1993). Processes that support shared leadership, decision making, and program evaluation (Jang & Mangione, 1994) as well as transition procedures that identify tasks, timelines, and responsibilities help staff plan for transition while reducing traditional barriers to planning and collaboration, such as disagreement about policy implementation and responsibilities, duplication of services, and lack of knowledge of other parts of the system (Rice & O'Brien, 1990).

Local service system factors refers to the current early childhood service delivery system, which includes numerous agencies and organizations within a community. These services and supports are unique to each community and are based on community priorities, concerns, and resources; therefore, various service system factors can have a positive or negative impact on the individual transition process for children, families, and providers (Rous, Hemmeter, & Schuster, 1994). The overall system model in place within the community and the various program models and array of options available to families must be considered as having potential implications for the transition process (Harbin et al., 2000). The need for collaboration across individual agencies in a community also has been identified as having an impact on transition (Rous, Hemmeter, & Schuster, 1999). Therefore, interagency linkages and interagency leadership (e.g., local interagency committees), as well as the resourcefulness of the community and community leaders, should be considered when exploring transition services and supports (Harbin et al., 2000; Salisbury et al., 1993).

Finally, *state factors* refers to the fact that state agencies are charged with general oversight and support for programs providing services to young children and families. The state plays a major role in the design of the service delivery model at the local level (Harbin et al., 2000, 2004). Leadership within the state can inhibit or facilitate the quality of services across the state and can provide the appropriate infrastructure to support quality practices, including state policy, technical assistance, and financial support (Harbin et al., 2004). As with the local level, the nature of communication and relationships across agencies at the state level can have an impact on the relationships among agencies at the local level. The state's overall commitment to young children and families and quality services also is a consideration (Harbin et al., 2000).

The Transition Process

The second level of the conceptual model provides specific information on the transition process, which is defined as the interaction among critical interagency variables, transition practices and activities, and immediate outcomes related to child and family preparation and adjustment (see Figure 2.2). The following describes the essential elements of these factors as they relate to the transition experiences of young children with disabilities and their families.

Critical Interagency Variables Transition is an interagency process that involves multiple parties such as families and various agencies. The proposed model identifies three critical variables that influence the quality and nature of the transition process. The first critical variable, communication and relationships, is grounded in the belief that the foundation of service delivery is the communication and relationships among people (Harbin et al., 2000; Thurman, 1997; Turnbull & Turnbull, 1997). Successful transitions in the early childhood years reflect processes that involve communication and relationships among the child, family, service providers, and agencies in the community (Pianta et al., 1999).

The second critical variable is a supportive interagency infrastructure, which must be in place to allow for relationship building and communication between and among agencies and families (Conn-Powers et al., 1990; Hanline, 1993; Harbin et al., 2000, 2004; Harbin & Salisbury, 2000; Rous et al., 1994, 1999). This infrastructure includes transition policies that are developed within and across programs that provide services, interagency agreements that outline specific roles and responsibilities for activities related to transition planning, and the formal and informal mechanisms that provide support for cross-agency communication and coordination (e.g., interagency councils).

The third critical variable is the alignment of programs and continuity of the service delivery system. The various providers of early childhood services operate within divergent funding sources, administration, policies, curriculum, and philosophies. Although programs do not have to be consistent across these dimensions for transition to be effective, an effective transition program supports continuity between programs among which families and children move. For example, attention to the types of learning experiences, the developmental appropriateness of the curriculum, and ensuring appropriate curriculum content and approaches are integral to the curriculum design in quality early childhood programs (Bredekamp & Copple, 1997). Therefore, a portion of transition planning success is based on continuity of the curriculum (Repetto & Correa, 1996).

Research suggests that the greater the continuity across programs, curricula, and personnel, the greater the likelihood for successful transition (Entwisle & Alexander, 1998). However, these discontinuities are numerous and can act as significant barriers to successful transition. These may include a poor match of curriculum (more academic at kindergarten than preschool), a more complex social environment in the next environment, less opportunity for parental involvement and support (particularly in the transition to kindergarten), less connections for and with families, and less time with the teacher (Pianta, Cox, Taylor, & Early, 1999). In addition, the alignment of therapeutic, health, and social services is of paramount importance as well. The discontinuity between the delivery and/or payment for therapy, health, and social services at transition is often cited as a powerful barrier to successful transitions. Program administrators and staff can further facilitate the transition process and ensure program continuity by providing developmentally appropriate curriculum for all age levels in all educational settings (Glicksman & Hills, 1981) and by engaging in strategies such as joint training and cross-program visits so that professionals can exchange information about expectations and experiences for children and make these more consistent (Pianta & Kraft-Sayre, 2003).

Transition Practices and Activities Some groups of practices and activities have been linked to successful and smooth transitions. These transition practices and activities typically address child-, family-, staff-, program-, and community-specific activities. For example, children are prepared for transition through participation in a variety of activities that allow them to learn about a new environment and through specific and intentional instruction/intervention to help them acquire the behaviors necessary to be successful in the next environment. Families and professionals share with children the expectation of the next environment. Families are supported through the transition process through frequent collaboration and communication with professionals to individualize transition planning and practices. A variety of practices must be offered and flexibly designed to meet the individual concerns of families (Pianta & Kraft-Sayre, 2003). Cross-program visits for families, staff, and children also play a vital role in helping build relationships, understanding, and knowledge across programs (Rous et al., 1994).

Although many practices enhance the transition process, other practices have been shown to inhibit or negatively affect the transition process, resulting in transitions that are frustrating and problematic (Harbin et al., 2000; Pianta & Cox, 1999). For example, in one national survey, kindergarten teachers indicated several barriers to successful transition planning. Some of these included not receiving their kindergarten rosters until school started, no administrative support or funds to make visits to kindergartners and their families during the summer prior to the start of school, and little, if any, opportunity to develop transition plans or engage in transition planning (Pianta et al., 1999).

Within the proposed conceptual framework, transition outcomes are defined as the level at which children and families are prepared for and adjust to the transition into a new environment. The following describes the essential elements of the preparation and adjustment process as they relate to the transition experiences of young children with disabilities and their families.

Child and Family Preparation The nature of the transition process (e.g., practices and activities) influences the effects of the critical variables on the preparation of the child and the family for the transition process. As children and families participate in the transition process, a number of transition activities can be implemented that support preparation for the transfer to new settings and/or services. Preparation of children and involvement of families in the transition process has been linked with more successful transition outcomes (Glicksman & Hills, 1981; Rous et al., 1999). As it relates to child preparation, the transition literature is replete with information regarding which specific skills should be targeted in an effort to ease the transition into preschool, kindergarten, and primary programs. These skills are typically categorized as 1) social and classroom conduct skills, 2) communication skills, 3) task-related skills, and 4) self-help skills (Chandler, 1993). In addition, skills and dispositions related to independence (e.g., communication with others), self-help skills, the ability to follow directions, and the ability to use materials appropriately also may be influential (Gamel-McCormick & Rous, 2000; Hemmeter & Rous, 1997; Johnson, Gallagher, Cook, & Wong, 1995; Rule, Fiechtl, & Innocenti, 1990). For children with special needs, teachers should focus specifically on child preparation to maximize prosocial and age-appropriate social skills and on responsiveness to various instructional styles and different environmental structures (Katims & Pierce, 1995).

Families should be involved early and often in the transition planning process. To support families' preparation, they must be seen as partners and primary decision makers in their children's care and education (Mangione & Speth, 1998), and classroom staff and interventionists should develop reciprocal relationships with parents (Bredekamp & Copple, 1997). In addition, supporting the parents' or caregivers' involvement in a child's learning and development (e.g., reading to the child, setting routines, using a positive approach to discipline, increasing the child's language skills) is linked to smoother transitions and improved outcomes (Pianta & Cox, 1999; Ramey & Ramey, 1998). Transition preparation involves providing information and activities that are idiosyncratic and based on family concerns (Chandler, 1993). Relationships with family members must be nurtured and respected as critical resources before, during, and after transition; and family strengths must be a focus of the transition practices (Pianta et al., 1999).

Child and Family Adjustment   The type of preparation for the transition process described previously can affect the nature of the adjustment of children and families. Children may be faced with very different environments and often have significant difficulties adjusting to new programs and activities (Kakvoulis, 1994). The research literature has provided significant data to suggest that a child's skill level in communication, engagement, and behavior heavily influences his or her ability to successfully transition and adjust to new environments (e.g., Gamel-McCormick & Rous, 2000; Johnson et al., 1995; Katims & Pierce, 1995). Therefore, the model acknowledges that the child's adjustment is the most proximal influence to child outcomes. However, the family's adjustment is believed to influence this important relationship between child adjustment and outcomes after transition. Families' access to knowledge and support during the transition process as well as their ability to advocate for their child's specific concerns during transition planning have been linked with more positive results (e.g., Byrd, Stephens, Dyk, Perry, & Rous, 1991; Jang & Mangione, 1994; Mangione & Speth, 1998; Meier & Schafran, 1999; Wheeler, Reetz, & Wheeler, 1993).

Child Success and Outcomes   As mentioned previously, the ultimate goal of transition planning is to ensure that children are successful in school and that they are able to achieve academic and social success. Therefore, the conceptual model proposes that these important child outcomes are most highly influenced by the child and family's adjustment to new programs. Ramey and Ramey (1994) provided some early markers of successful transitions that included very specific outcomes related to children, such as a positive attitude about school (e.g., children like school and look forward to going to school regularly) and steady growth in academic skills. Family outcomes include parents and guardians who are actively involved in their child's education and who value school (Ramey & Ramey, 1994).

IMPLICATIONS

Since the mid-1980s, progress has been made toward the identification of scientifically based practices associated with successful transitions for young children and their families. The literature primarily has focused on the mechanics of effective transition procedures, but little is available on the complex interactions among the components at all levels of the ecology and the influences on child success during and after transitions. Although the evidence in the literature is fragmented, it shows organizational complexities and the resulting problems experienced by families, children, and in many instances, the professionals who provide services. Research suggests that addressing the child's entire ecological context is essential in planning and implementing effective transitions (Pianta & Walsh, 1996); however, practice has focused primarily on child skills and abilities (Meisels, 1999; Rimm-Kaufmann & Pianta, 1999).

Consequently, federal monitoring reports and state evaluations indicate that transitions have been and continue to be extremely problematic, and it is often the component of service delivery with which families are least satisfied (Kochanek, Costa, McGinn, & Cummins, 1997). Therefore, if the experiences and outcomes of those involved in transitions are to be improved, service providers need to understand 1) the complex interactions and relationships among variables in the ecology, 2) how these complex interactions are linked to the child's success in school, 3) if the factors and their interrelationships are the same for the transitions at different times, and 4) how to address populations that are likely to experience the most difficulty during and after transitions.

Chapter **3**

Building the Interagency Team

In Hobart County, a small rural community, a local interagency team has been in existence for about 10 years. This interagency group meets monthly to share information about services as well as to consider and plan for potential shared activities. They work together on Child Find issues and have developed a community resource guide for both families and providers.

• • •

In Metroville, a large urban community, several interagency groups exist to coordinate services for children and families; unfortunately, in the past, services and referrals have gotten lost in the shuffle. However, a task force recently has been established to focus on the transition of preschoolers to kindergarten. Representatives from the local public schools, the health department, the local child care resource and referral group, Head Start, and community-based mental health programs have met biweekly over the past year to develop and begin to implement a plan to improve transitions to kindergarten in the community. The initiation of spring preschool meetings has been one strategy used by this task force to increase parent knowledge of kindergarten and to help families gain access to services prior to kindergarten entry. This local task force is also working to examine the different curricula used throughout the preschool and kindergarten programs in an effort to enhance program practices throughout the community and to improve child outcomes.

• • •

Communities often develop ways in which representatives from different agencies can get together to plan around common issues—in this case transition. This chapter focuses on helping agencies in a community build an interagency team whose sole focus is to develop transition processes that are congruent across agencies and programs, congruent in that planning efforts and processes work in harmony and support one another as opposed to transition processes that are incompatible and often contradictory in nature.

Interagency teams often already are established in communities that focus on issues for young children and families. Due to the complexities of the transition process (as described in Chapter 2), however, building effective teams often requires focused attention and special efforts. Establishing an interagency transition team can provide the structure and support needed to address transition issues on a collaborative basis, therefore supporting congruency across the system.

THE NEED FOR INTERAGENCY COLLABORATION

Early childhood programs, as with most human services programs, are often stretched to meet a growing need for services in a time of continually shrinking resources. Collaboration across early childhood programs and agencies offers an opportunity for these programs and agencies to come together to work toward a common purpose or goal and utilize shared financial and interpersonal resources (Kagan, 1992). This, in turn, helps ensure that children and families receive the variety of supports that may be necessary to meet their needs and offers a structure through which agencies can maximize resources and prevent duplication of services. For example, a child and family may be receiving mental health services as part of the Head Start program that they attend in the morning but may also be receiving similar services through referral from the Family Resource Center that is housed in the public preschool program they attend in the afternoon. Collaboration across agencies can enhance services in a number of areas. These areas include the screening and identification of children who are at risk for or who have disabilities, the provision of therapeutic and educational services to children in community-based settings, the coordination of health and mental health services for children who are in early care and education programs, and the provision of an array of family supports to enhance a child's optimal growth and development. The need for collaboration is particularly important as children transition among agencies because this has been shown to be a time of high stress for both families and children (Karr-Jelinek, 1994; Rosenkoetter, Hains, & Fowler, 1994).

To underscore the importance of transition planning on a collaborative basis, many federal programs require collaborative transition planning among relevant agencies. For example, Head Start, programs for children with disabil-

Table 3.1.   Head Start transition requirements

Disability Service Plan-45 C.F.R. 1308 (Subpart B)
   For grantees, not individual children
   Procedures for transition from early intervention to early education or other next placement
   Preparation of parents and staff for the transition
   Interagency agreements as appropriate to support coordination of services and transition
   Screening and referrals
Performance Standards-45 C.F.R. 1304-A
   Refer to Local Education Agency for evaluation (Subpart D)

From National Early Childhood Transition Center. (2005). *IDEA 2004 & early childhood transition.* Lexington, KY: Interdisciplinary Human Development Institute. Available online at www.ihdi.uky.edu/NECTC/idea2004; reprinted by permission.

ities under the Individuals with Disabilities Education Improvement Act (IDEA) of 2004 (PL 108-446), and the No Child Left Behind Act of 2001 (PL 107-110) have specific recommendations or mandates for transition that include interagency collaboration through interagency agreements, policies, and procedures (see Table 3.1, Table 3.2, and Figure 3.1).

Establishing a Community-Based Interagency Transition Team

The nature and design of early care and education programs is divergent and complex. Services often are offered through a variety of organizations, such as health care organizations, human services agencies, and education systems. Different communities offer different programs. Even when the same program type is offered in different communities (e.g., state preschool, Head Start), the programs themselves often have unique cultures and administrative and operational structures. This culture and structure are shaped by many factors, such as the size of the community or the leadership within the agencies and programs. For example, in one community, the superintendent of the public school system may feel strongly that collaboration among agencies is essential to quality services. Therefore, she may encourage and support interagency activities and events. In another community, the superintendent may feel strongly that the school system is responsible for meeting the educational needs of children

Table 3.2.   No Child Left Behind transition requirements

Emphasizes coordination between Head Start, Early Reading First, and other early childhood programs and the public schools, especially

• Receiving records with parent consent
• Establishing channels of communication
• Conducting meetings to discuss the needs of individual children
• Organizing and participating in joint transition-related training of personnel
• Linking educational services

From National Early Childhood Transition Center. (2005). *IDEA 2004 & early childhood transition.* Lexington, KY: Interdisciplinary Human Development Institute. Available online at www.ihdi.uky.edu/NECTC/idea2004; reprinted by permission.

Part C/Early intervention (EI) services for infants and toddlers	Part B/Early childhood special education (ECSE) services for preschool children
State plan	
Interagency agreements with state education agency for Part B	Interagency agreements with lead agency for Part C and Head Start
State policies include Child Find, flexible funding, and staff development.	State policies include Child Find and use of individualized family service plan (IFSP) services, which begin at age 3.
	For those children who participated in Part C, states can choose to provide early intervention services for children up to kindergarten entry rather than enrolling in Part B section 619 services.
Transition conference	
The transition conference is to include representatives of the EI agency, the ECSE agency, and the family.	A local education agency representative must participate in the transition conference hosted by Part C.
A transition conference must be held for all children in Part C at least 90 days and up to 6 months prior to age 3.	The Part C service coordinator or other representative should be invited to the initial individualized education program (IEP) meeting at the request of the parent.

Figure 3.1. Comparison of IDEA transition requirements for Part C and Part B programs. (From National Early Childhood Transition Center. [2005]. *IDEA 2004 & early childhood transition*. Lexington, KY: Interdisciplinary Human Development Institute. Available online at www.ihdi.uky.edu/NECTC/idea2004; adapted by permission.)

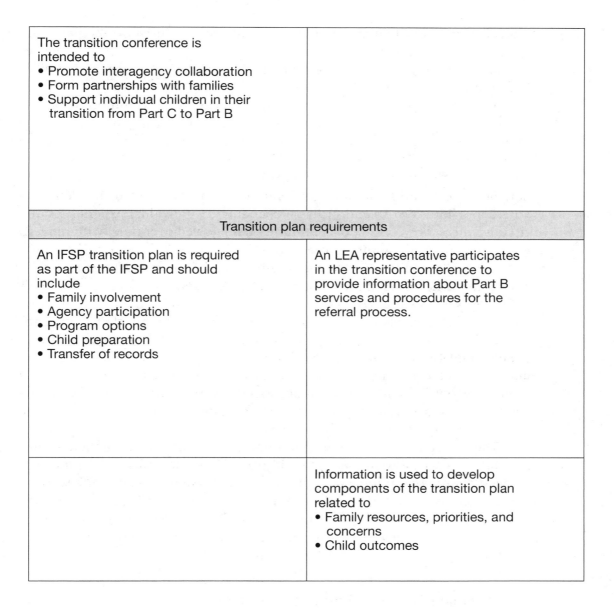

The transition conference is intended to • Promote interagency collaboration • Form partnerships with families • Support individual children in their transition from Part C to Part B	
Transition plan requirements	
An IFSP transition plan is required as part of the IFSP and should include • Family involvement • Agency participation • Program options • Child preparation • Transfer of records	An LEA representative participates in the transition conference to provide information about Part B services and procedures for the referral process.
	Information is used to develop components of the transition plan related to • Family resources, priorities, and concerns • Child outcomes

and their families but not—given limited resources—their social and emotional needs. Therefore, this superintendent may not support programs that link families to needed social services agencies such as the family resource center.

Because programs and services differ from community to community, transition issues and barriers also differ. The key stakeholders involved in transition planning, as well as the strategies and practices that are implemented to address issues and barriers, may differ from community to community as well. This does not mean that common stakeholders or issues and barriers do not exist across communities. It does mean that strategies and practices that are common across communities and even states must be tailored to meet the individual needs of that community and must be responsive to the particular agencies and programs that offer services in that community. These strategies and practices also must meet the unique needs of staff, children, and families in a community.

To this end, the heart of the transition process is the community, that is, defining the community and the key stakeholders that will participate in the interagency transition team. Therefore, to address the transition needs of the children and families served through these programs at a community level, the concept of community must be understood. Most people consider themselves part of some type of community. Community can be defined in relation to where individuals work and/or live, depending on individual experiences and circumstances. The concept of community has evolved over time, with modern efforts to define community traced to 1887 and the work of Ferdinand Tonnies. Tonnies introduced the idea of community being more than *kinship* and *place*, adding the concepts of shared value systems and common interests. Tonnies's definition suggests that communities are dynamic entities that are influenced by the people and relationships that exist within them rather than static entities defined solely by geographic boundaries. Bellah, Madsen, Sullivan, Swidler, and Tipton (1985) added the concept of memory to the definition and description of community. Bellah and colleagues defined community as "a group of people who are socially independent, who participate together in discussion and decision making, and who share certain practices that both define community and are nurtured by it" (1985, p. 55).

The first step in the process of transition planning is defining the community for which transition planning will occur. In some areas, community includes a county or a number of counties in a geographic region that have similar characteristics and programs. In other areas, community may mean a large city that includes multiple programs and agencies. As an interagency team defines community, they should consider two distinct characteristics: 1) demographics and economy and 2) service systems.

Demographics and Economy   As community is defined in terms of transition planning, the influence of demographics and economy on both the development of the community team and transition is important to understand. Community demographics play a large role in defining the number and types of programs that will be in place for young children and their families. For example, large urban areas generally have many more options for child care than rural areas. Communities that rely on blue-collar industries for viability may influence the hours of operation of child care facilities to accommodate third shift employees. Communities that have higher percentages of families of lower socioeconomic status (SES) may have more programs geared toward at-risk individuals than their affluent neighboring communities. The distinctive service delivery system based on these demographic and economic factors that have developed in a particular community will certainly influence the community transition process and the nature of the interagency relationships in that community.

Service Systems In addition to the influence of demographics and economics on the nature and types of services offered within communities, the different approaches to service delivery also are a factor in the need for community-based transition planning. When considering the design of early care and education systems in local communities, two primary fields of practice affect the delivery of services to young children: early childhood education and early childhood special education. Families and children who participate in early childhood special education are entitled to services once they have met specific criteria for eligibility. In early childhood programs, this is not always the case. Even in programs that have eligibility criteria, such as Head Start, the current resources and funding of the program may result in only a percentage of eligible children actually receiving services.

Although not all children who are at risk or who have disabilities or delays are identified during the early childhood period, the number of children participating in early care and education programs has grown since the 1980s. Many states have expanded programs that serve young children, implementing programs that are universal or programs that serve targeted populations. At the same time, funding for early childhood programs that receive federal support (e.g., Head Start and services for children with disabilities) has also been expanded, but not at a pace that has kept up with the increasing enrollment in those programs or at a pace that ensures that all eligible children and families receive the services that they need (U.S. Department of Education, 2003). In addition, although many states have increased their investment in early care and education programs through state-funded preschool, the changing demographics in the United States, such as rising poverty rates for women and children and increases in transient populations, have resulted in an increased need in services. Unfortunately, the current level of funding for early childhood program in states has not been able to adequately respond to this increased need (Ramey & Ramey, 1998).

Identifying Key Stakeholders for the Interagency Team

Once the community has been defined, the next step is to identify key stakeholder agencies that will be represented on the interagency team. The makeup of the interagency team should include key stakeholder agencies and programs that 1) have responsibility for transition planning (through state or federal mandates and regulations) at both the sending and receiving ends and 2) are major players in the delivery of services to young children and families. The goal of this interagency team is to focus specifically on transition issues and concerns within the community. Figure 3.2 (also provided as a blank form on page 167

Program/service	Your community program/service name(s)
Early intervention	Early Steps
• Point of entry into system	Southeast Regional Early Intervention District
• Service coordination	Southeast Child Development Center
Public school	Metroville Schools
• Preschool	East Metroville Early Childhood Center
• Preschool special education	Metroville Schools District Office
• Even Start	Metroville Schools District Office
• Title I	Metroville Schools District Office
• Kindergarten/primary program	East Metroville Elementary
Head Start	Southeast Community Services Center, Highland Head Start
Early Head Start	Southeast Community Services Center, Highland Head Start
Public health	Metroville Regional Medical Board, Healthy Start
Mental health	Southeast Community Services Center, Early Childhood Mental Health Services
Social services	Southeast Community Services Center
Child care	Little Lambs and 3C, Southeast Coordinated Child Care Resource and Referral
Specialized intervention programs	Southeast Services for the Visually Impaired, Statewide Deaf-Blind Program

Figure 3.2. Survey: Agencies and programs to include in the transition-planning process (sample).

in the appendix) can be used to help identify the specific agencies or programs that provide services to young children in the community and that should be included in the transition planning process. At this point, the goal is not to determine specific individuals within agencies that should participate as part of the team; rather, the goal is to determine those agencies, programs, or services that need to be represented on the team.

After generating a list of programs and services, the second step is to determine if interagency groups exist in the identified list of key stakeholders that already are addressing transition or that may provide support to transition-planning efforts. For example, some of the key stakeholders may already meet on a regular basis to coordinate services for children with disabilities or participate in a Success by Six program. Both of these groups should have a vested interest in the transition process and may already be addressing transition issues in the community. The flowchart in Figure 3.3 can be used to help determine whether the transition process presented in this book can be integrated with an existing interagency group or a new interagency group should be established.

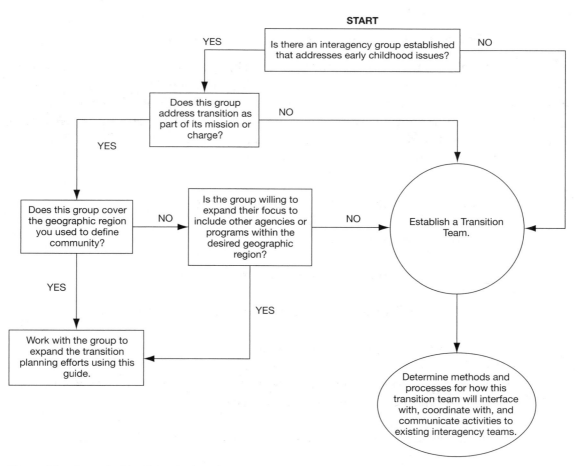

Figure 3.3. Steps for identifying the interagency transition team.

The next step is to hold an initial meeting with key stakeholders to begin the community transition-planning process. At this point, someone should take primary responsibility for issuing invitations and determining the agenda for this meeting. This person will provide leadership until the group decides on an organizational structure for the group. To begin this process, this person should read Chapter 4, which can assist him or her in developing the initial agenda and process for the first meeting. A sample invitation for the initial meeting is provided in Figure 3.4.

The first meeting of the transition team should be devoted to laying the groundwork for future work. This involves two phases. In Phase 1, the group must answer three critical questions about the status of transition in the community. Based on the outcome of group discussion and the responses to these three questions, Phase 2 involves making two key decisions that will begin the process of community planning. A sample agenda that outlines these critical steps for the first meeting (filled in for Hobart County Schools) is provided in Figure 3.5. A blank copy of this form is provided on page 168 in the appendix.

Phase 1: Considering Three Critical Questions

What do we mean by transition? The group must have a common understanding of what transition is. Within the model presented in this book, the authors define this transition as a process of movement or change from one environment to another. This movement or change in programs or services brings new opportunities and challenges for staff, families, and children. Therefore, within this definition, transitions include the following:

1. Changes in programs, including moving from

   • The hospital to home

   • The home to child care or early intervention

   • An early intervention program to a preschool program

   • A preschool program to school

2. Changes in the curriculum style and structure between programs, classrooms, and the teacher or related-services personnel

3. Changes in the program, classroom, or therapeutic philosophy

4. Changes in providers, teachers, and staff

Dear Ms. Alexander:

We are interested in starting a community-based transition team to address specific transition issues in our area. The purpose of the transition team will be to develop a long-range transition plan that can be implemented across agencies and programs that serve young children and families.

The development of a community-based transition team in our area is an important step to ensure that young children have the support they need to make transitions among the various programs in our area and to support their eventual transition to school. Research has shown that children's success in school is enhanced through quality services and transition supports in the early years. In addition, the requirements related to transition for children in Head Start programs and for young children with disabilities serviced through the Individuals with Disabilities Education Improvement Act of 2004 and as specified in the No Child Left Behind Act of 2001, provide the impetus for us to think about how to address the issue of transition in a way that is coordinated across agencies. As part of our work, we plan to create a transition team that integrates with existing councils and networks in our community.

Our first community transition team meeting is scheduled for:
Date and time: <u>October 23, 2006</u>   Location: <u>Hobart Head Start Center</u>

Please use the attached RSVP to let us know if you can attend. Hope to see you at the meeting!

Sincerely,

Robert Halloway

Robert Halloway

- -

Community Transition Team Meeting RSVP

Name: Title:

Agency:

Address:

Phone: Fax:

E-mail:

I can attend: ☐ Yes   ☐ No

☐ I cannot attend but am interested in participating in future transition team
    meetings.

Please return by: October 16, 2006

Figure 3.4.   Invitation to initial meeting (sample).

Initial Meeting Agenda

Topic/time allotted	Action/process	Materials	Facilitator/ discussant
Welcome/ introductions (15 minutes)	Introduce and provide an overview of the purpose of the meeting.	Name tags	Mary Sue
Agenda and process overview (15 minutes)	Present agenda and process to be used during the meeting; revise as appropriate.	Topical agenda on flip chart Markers Paper copies of agenda	Mary
Phase 1 (45 minutes)	Present/discuss three critical questions: 1. What is transition? Team develops transition definition. 2. What do we believe about transition? Group reflects individually, has a discussion, and generates guiding principles. 3. What is the status of transition in our community? Team decides whether there is a need for a community transition team.	Flip chart Worksheet pages Markers Post-It notes	Sue
Phase 2 (1 hour)	Present/discuss two key decisions: 1. What is the scope of our transition system? Group determines age and characteristics of children for whom transition planning will occur. 2. Who is missing from the table? Group discusses other agencies or representatives that need to be invited to participate and how families can be involved.	Flip chart Worksheet pages Markers	Mary
Next steps/ agenda building (15 minutes)	Group reviews decisions. Group determines agenda for next meeting, including time and location of next meeting. Group determines tasks that need to be accomplished before the next meeting and assigns tasks. The group adjourns.		Sue

Figure 3.5.   Initial meeting agenda. Sample: Hobart County, USA.

As a community, coming to agreement on how transition is defined is important. This definition will set the foundation for the specific planning process and key stakeholders for the group. For example, the Hobart County team defined transition as a process of moving between and among agencies, programs, and services.

What do we believe about transition?   The next step is to agree on a set of guiding principles about transition. This includes a series of statements that outline group beliefs about the transition process. These belief statements will form the guiding principles that the team will use throughout the planning process. To establish these principles, the group should start by allowing each team member to list his or her individual beliefs about transition. To start the process, the group facilitator may present the group with a starter statement (e.g., "I believe that transition. . . ."). Group members can write individual belief statements on Post-It notes that are collected by the facilitator or placed in a basket or bowl.

Once the group members have had an opportunity to reflect individually, individual belief statements can be read aloud and consolidated into like comments and beliefs. These beliefs then form the basis, through group discussion, of a common set of guiding principles. Sample guiding principles for the Metroville transition team are presented in Figure 3.6.

What is the status of transition within our community?   Using the list of guiding principles, the group can then determine whether these guiding principles are in evidence across the represented agencies and programs. In other words, are the group members practicing transition in a way that accurately reflects what they believe transition should be? This is a crucial point for the group. If the answer is yes, then it is difficult for the group to see a need for a community transition team and the continuation of the process. If the answer is no, then the group has identified a reason to think about addressing transition in a new way and should proceed to the next phase of transition planning. Again, Phase 2 presents two critical questions to begin the process of community planning.

Phase 2: Two Critical Decisions

What transition points do we want to address?   The first decision involves determining the scope of the transition system that will be developed by the community team. This involves identifying the transition points to be addressed by the group, including the age range to be covered and characteristics of the young children and families who will be the focus of transition planning. For example, the Metroville team may choose to focus on the transition of young children from birth to their entry into the primary program (first grade). Within this age range, the group may feel that they should focus specifically on

---

Metroville Team Guiding Principles:
1. Children and families are at the center of all transition planning efforts.
2. Families and staff are involved in designing transition systems and services.
3. The transition process requires an interagency focus, collaboration among providers within the community, and attention to relationships among providers and agencies.
4. Transition is a process and not an event.

Figure 3.6.   Transition team guiding principles. Sample: Metroville, USA.

Scope of Transitions Checklist	

Transition points	Characteristics
☑ Hospital to home ☑ Into infant/toddler services ☑ Into preschool ☐ Into kindergarten ☐ Into primary school (e.g., first grade) ☐ Into intermediate school (e.g., fourth grade)	☐ Children with specific disabilities (e.g., significant disabilities; visual impairments) ☑ Children with all identified disabilities ☑ Children at risk for disabilities ☑ Children at risk (e.g., poverty, abuse) ☐ All children

Figure 3.7. Checklist: scope of transitions (sample).

children who have disabilities or they may focus on all young children. The Scope of Transitions checklist in Figure 3.7 can help the group determine its focus. (See page 169 for the photocopiable form.)

Depending on the focus on which the group decides, the group will need to identify the specific legal requirements that will help shape the thinking of the group during planning efforts.

What key stakeholders are we missing? Once the scope of the system to be designed has been determined, the team is ready to refine the list of participants who need to be included in the process. At this point, the specific agencies and the people within those agencies who can ensure that the scope of the transition system is addressed in future planning should be identified. As Figure 3.8 shows, the Hobart County team identified six specific agencies

Transition Team Participants	

Agency name	Which staff positions need to be involved?
Early intervention program	Local program director, local Interagency Coordinating Council chair, regional office staff
Public school	Preschool coordinator, regional special education cooperative director, principal
Local health department	Early childhood mental health consultant, Healthy Start consultant
Head Start program	Director, disability specialist/coordinator
Family resource center	Director
Child care	Director

Figure 3.8. Transition team participants. Sample: Hobart County, USA.

Involving Families	
Given our scope, which transition points should be represented?	Three-year-old with special needs transition, 5–year-old with special needs transition, kindergarten transition for all kids
How many family members should be included on the team?	One at each transition point
How will families be supported in their participation?	A stipend will be provided to families for participation in monthly meetings.

Figure 3.9.   Involving families. Sample: Metroville, USA.

that they thought were critical to their transition process. Figure 3.8 (a blank copy of which is provided on page 170 in the appendix) can be helpful in identifying agencies with which young children and their families are most commonly involved in transition (e.g., early intervention, public schools, Head Start, child care, mental health/mental retardation) so that a comprehensive and coordinated system can be put in place. This system would help to determine staff positions in these agencies comprised of individuals who could contribute knowledge about the transition process and/or staff positions that will be most critical during the transition system design process.

After agency representatives have been determined, the team should consider the extent to which families of young children can be involved in the transition system design and operation. This is especially important if the guiding principles developed by the team indicated that families are essential members of the planning team. If the team determines that family members will participate as members of the transition team, they will then have to decide in what capacity they will participate and how they will be supported. Figure 3.9—filled in for Hobart County Schools—can help the team determine levels of family involvement. For example, should family members be representative of specific transition points, such as a family member who has already experienced the transition process at age 3 or 5, and if so, how will the team identify these families and the role they will play? A blank copy of Figure 3.9 is provided on page 171 in the appendix.

DEVELOPING A VISION FOR TRANSITION

Once the transition team has been formed and understands the scope of its work, the team needs to establish a vision of what transition should look like that can be shared by all of the participants in the transition system (see Figure

Developing a Vision	
Audience	**Goals of effective transition planning**
Young children	Be timely. Address children's individual needs. Reduce time without services or supports.
Families	Include families as members of the team. Address transition concerns and needs of families. Be coordinated and nonduplicative.
Providers/teachers and other staff	Include effective transition planning as part of my job requirements. Include activities that have been shown to be effective. Be supported by my supervisor and agency. Be coordinated across agencies.
Administrators	Help me ensure that I am meeting legal requirements. Be coordinated to reduce duplication and wasted resources. Start early and include all transition points.

Figure 3.10. Developing a vision. Sample: Metroville, USA.

3.10). The vision statement, once defined, presents the big picture and represents the ultimate goal of the transition planning process. Establishing vision statements can be a difficult and sometimes tedious process; therefore, the following guidelines are recommended:

1. The vision should be developed by identifying the characteristics of the transition system that the team collectively wants to establish. Different people in the system will have varying perspectives on what characteristics are important; therefore, start by asking people to work independently and then to use a process of discussion and consolidation to identify those characteristics on which all stakeholders can agree.

2. As the team starts the vision development process, team members should identify key words and phrases that represent their desired characteristics. Do not try to write sentences. The team should not wordsmith at this point. The point is to capture the essence of the desired characteristics.

3. Keep in mind the scope of the community transition system that the team is developing. It will help if the team facilitator posts the transition definitions and scope arrived at earlier in the team-building process on flip chart paper on the wall as team members work through this process.

4. Once established, this vision should become the cornerstone for decision making across all aspects of the transition-planning process.

In Hobart County, children from birth to age 5 and their families will receive quality, seamless services provided by agencies throughout the area working together. Children and families are our focus.

• • •

The Metroville transition team will focus on developing a partnership between families and service providers that enhances the transition process for children with developmental disabilities. We will concentrate on providing a smooth transition for children between birth and 5 years of age who are entering an educational system. Through a cooperative effort, agencies will strive to serve as transition resources and expand options to continually meet the changing needs of children and families.In Hobart County, children from birth to age 5 and their families will receive quality, seamless services provided by agencies throughout the area working together. Children and families are our focus.

Figure 3.11. Hobart County and Metroville community vision statements.

5. The Figure 3.10 worksheet can assist the team as they begin to identify key characteristics by helping them to think about the multiple audiences—young children, families, local education agencies, social services agencies—for which the transition process should be developed. A blank copy of this worksheet is provided on page 172 in the appendix at the end of this book.

With a set of agreed-on, desired characteristics in hand, the next step is to develop a congruent statement that the full group will adopt. It usually works out well to have a small subgroup of team members work on a potential vision statement that includes the key characteristics agreed on by the team. The subgroup can then bring the vision statement back to the group for input and a final decision. One approach that has been successful for many teams is to present the statement and have individual team members identify specific words or phrases that they cannot live with. The team can then negotiate other words or phrases to complete the statement. During this discussion, the team should have copies of the transition definition, scope, and key characteristics posted on flip chart paper on the wall as a reference for the group. The final vision statements for Hobart County and Metroville are presented in Figure 3.11.

This chapter presents steps and strategies for identifying key stakeholders in the transition process and developing consensus around the overall goal and vision of the team in supporting more successful transitions among agencies and programs. By implementing these steps, the community can systematically build a transition team that has the greatest potential for a positive impact on the transition process for young children.

Chapter 4

Interagency Structure

Claire, the chair of the Metroville interagency transition team, is frustrated. The team has been working for 6 months now on getting a plan in place to support some of the activities they are interested in implementing to address their transition problems. She was so excited when they finally identified the agency representatives to sit on the team, but now that they have the names, everything seems to be falling apart. First, it seems that different people are attending the meetings every month. This means that Claire spends most of the meeting time bringing people up to speed before they can move forward. Second, when they do make decisions, they seem to revisit them the next time they are together. She needs help!

• • •

The community transition process is heavily influenced by the ability of community agencies to work and make decisions together as an interagency group. Interagency collaboration is a common need in most community initiatives. With the greater number and types of services available to young children and their families comes the need for more extensive and effective collaboration between the agencies providing these services. Implementing community-based initiatives can be both rewarding and challenging. Few would argue that collaboration among agencies in supporting young children and families is a worthy and laudable goal. In fact, numerous studies have been conducted, books have been written, and resources have been developed to help agencies work together more effectively to implement services. However, the increasing demands on agencies for higher levels of service in terms of quantity and quality, the recent focus on accountability for results, and limited financial and personnel resources serve to increase the need for strategies that make collaborative planning both effective and efficient. Using several important components of the collaborative community-building process, including communication and relationship building (e.g., Breznay, 2001; Page, 2003) as well as participation and consultation of various community members (e.g., Fawcett, 2003; Flaspohler, 2003), this chapter provides information on specific strategies for developing an interagency structure to support effective community planning initiatives.

As evidenced by the previous vignette, an effective interagency structure can support the team in how to work together to accomplish its goals and objectives, whereas a team without a formal structure can leave participants frustrated. A good interagency structure includes formal decisions about how the group will operate, the rules under which it will function, and the ways in which the team will continually build its capacity to make decisions and implement activities. The interagency structure sets the framework for how the group will work together to accomplish its vision. There are three key components of the interagency structure that help make the interagency planning process successful:

1. Understanding team building and the development process

2. Establishing a clear operational structure for effective participation across agencies

3. Developing a meeting structure that supports planning efforts

EFFECTIVE TEAMS AND TEAM DEVELOPMENT

In community transition planning, a *team* is defined as a group of people who are working together toward a common goal or outcome. Developing effective teams requires commitment on the part of all team members. This process starts with understanding what an effective team looks like, determining where the team is currently functioning, and taking steps to build team success over time. Chapter 3 provided specific information on establishing the interagency team, including how to identify key stakeholders. Once the team is identified, the following characteristics of effective teams (Francis & Young,

1992)—structure and discipline, focus and productivity, conflict, synergy, team growth, and individual growth—are particularly applicable for developing communitywide transition systems.

Structure and Discipline

Teams need to attend to the process of their meetings as well as the content of their meetings. They do this by establishing a meeting structure and ground rules to govern the work of the group. For example, when making decisions, the outcome of the decision-making process is important because it provides directions about where the team needs to go next. However, the process used to make the decision is also critical as it has the potential to affect the willingness of the team to stick with and support the decision. If a team member were to believe that the decision-making process was unfair or biased, then he or she potentially would not be as committed to the final decision. Therefore, the team should follow guidelines that have been established by the group and show a willingness to update processes and guidelines as needed to enhance the team's functioning.

Focus and Productivity

All teams should have clearly defined goals and objectives that are mutually desirable across team members. However, the effectiveness of the team is enhanced when team members have the capacity to actually produce desirable outcomes, including processes and products based on these goals and objectives. In other words, teams need to see action as a result of their work. When teams are focused and are able to develop products and/or make specific recommendations related to actions to be taken by their agency, following up on the implementation of these actions is critical to maintaining team focus and continuing to work together effectively.

Conflict

Each team member should feel free to offer his or her perspectives and opinions related to the work of the group, strategies under consideration, and the ways in which the group is working together without fear of reprisal from fellow team members. Remember that conflict is not necessarily negative if it is welcomed by the team and results in better outcomes. William E. Channing, (1780–1842) said, "Difficulties are meant to rouse, not discourage. The human spirit is to grow strong by conflict." However, equally important is for the team to agree on a shared method of problem solving in the group. This includes establishing steps and processes for how the group will handle problems that do not seem to have a ready solution.

Synergy

Each team member brings personal and professional strengths and experiences to the table that enhance the work of the group. However, the team's effectiveness depends on capitalizing on each member's individual energy to collectively enhance the power of the group. In other words, the whole can be stronger than the individual parts. Working together, the team can better capitalize on the energy of the group to accomplish the goals and objectives set forth by them as a team.

Team Growth

As the team works through specific issues and begins to accomplish particular tasks, team members can develop new strategies and techniques to work better together as a team. This learning process evolves through honest group discussion about how well the team is functioning and then by trying new strategies as needed. To this end, effective teams provide support to individual team members, and their interactions demonstrate respect and trust between each member of the group.

Individual Growth

Although team growth is important, the individual growth and fulfillment of each member is necessary if the individuals are to continue to participate actively. Effective teams understand that its individual members need to be able to grow both personally and professionally through their involvement in the team processes. Shared leadership, active participation, and shared responsibility across team members help support individual growth.

STAGES OF TEAM DEVELOPMENT

The Hobart County transition team really has been plugging along on the community transition plan over the past year. However, 3 months ago, the Head Start representative, Mary, took another job and left the team. The new Head Start representative,

Jill, is a nice person, but since she joined the team, the team seems to be floundering and cannot seem to get back to where they were before Mary left.

• • •

Four stages of team development were originally proposed by Tuckman in 1965: forming, storming, norming, and performing. The transition team can use these stages of team development to track and support their progress and to help assess the team's effectiveness and levels of functioning within the team. For example, on an annual basis, the team can use the stages of team development, illustrated in Figure 4.1, to reflect on where the team currently is in the development process and/or on the specific stages they have been through over the course of the year. However, as the previous vignette shows, teams commonly move among the various stages, especially as membership changes in the team.

Stage 1: Forming

The team comes together for the first time in the forming stage. During this time, each team member must determine his or her specific place and function

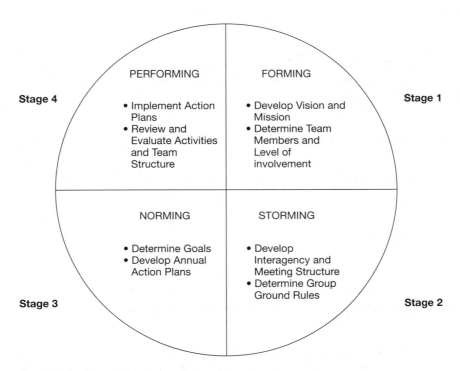

Figure 4.1.   Stages of team development.

in the group by considering this set of questions, either consciously or unconsciously:

- Where do I fit in this group?

- What am I doing here?

- What role am I expected to take?

For new teams, members go through the forming stage together. This is an opportune time for the team to develop a common vision and mission statement so that each team member has the opportunity to participate in the process to see where he or she fits in the group and what role he or she can play in realizing the vision. As new members join the group, they—just like Jill from Hobart County in the previous vignette—must go through this stage of team development so that they understand where they fit into an already organized team. They must also have an opportunity to understand the vision, mission, and goals already developed by the group (see Chapter 3) to see where they fit into the team.

Stage 2: Storming

Effective teams understand the importance of structure and discipline in the team process. The storming stage is when processes are developed and/or refined by the team. Team members must determine issues of structure and control in the group; this process of sharing divergent opinions sets the scene for future interactions and determines the culture of the group. Questions that may arise are

- Who controls this team? An individual? The whole group?

- How is control exercised within this team? Through force? Persuasion? Consensus?

- What rules does the team operate under?

- What happens to those who do not follow the rules of the group?

For new teams, this is the time when team members will negotiate the processes and ground rules under which their work will be accomplished. Specific decisions about leadership, meeting structure, and decision-making processes to be used by the group will be made during this stage. Once the structure of the group has been decided and recorded, information can be shared with new members to help orient the new members into the group culture and facilitate their participation in the group.

Stage 3: Norming

Once the team members understand their roles and the group has a structure in place to support group processes, the team is ready to take action. During this stage, the team should use the team tools and structure put in place to set goals and develop action plans that will guide the work of the group. Questions the team may face include

- What goals do we want to set?

- How do the goals fit with our vision and mission?

- What does our action plan need to look like?

During the norming stage, the team should decide the overall course and select long-term goals as a group; however, the team members may determine that they would benefit from breaking into subgroups or from working in smaller teams to accomplish specific tasks and actions.

Stage 4: Performing

This final stage of team development represents a team that is functioning well and is able to accomplish the work of the group effectively and efficiently. During this stage of development, the team is able to reach key decisions and produce desired outcomes that are valued and implemented by all team members. At this stage of the process, team members need to be vigilant, to continually assess their functioning, and to be willing to respond to any signs that team functioning is deteriorating, addressing issues quickly.

The goal of this book is to provide the community with steps and strategies for building a transition system that supports the team in working through the stages of team development and that results in a team that is able to reach Stage 4—the performing stage. However, one important thing to remember about team stages is that they change as membership in the group changes. As new members join a team, the team will naturally go back through the stages of development with the new members. This process takes time, so teams should try to minimize the changes in team membership and develop strategies for quickly orienting new team members when they do join the group. Specific strategies include

- Develop an orientation packet for new members that describe the team structure, processes, and ground rules as well as the current goals, objectives, and activities for the group.

- Establish a mentoring system so that new members receive information about the group prior to their first meeting. It is usually helpful for an outgoing member to serve as a mentor for an incoming member, especially if the two members represent the same agency or organization.

ESTABLISHING AN EFFECTIVE STRUCTURE FOR OPERATION AND PARTICIPATION ACROSS AGENCIES

Because of the often shifting responsibilities of agency personnel, expecting each team member to maintain the same level of involvement in all activities proposed and implemented by the transition team across time can be difficult. In fact, the level of involvement of members of the transition team should vary according to their roles, level of interest, and experience with the particular action in which the team is involved. At times, an activity that is taken on by the team clearly affects some agencies more than others. For example, the team may determine that children with disabilities who turn 3 during the summer are not receiving timely services. This activity may affect the disability programs for infants and toddlers, the public preschool program for children with disabilities, and Head Start programs more significantly than it would a local child care or a school-age public school program. Therefore, allowing members of the team to change their level of involvement will keep them interested in the process and allow them to focus their energies and talents appropriately. Expecting all members of the team to continue the same level of involvement over time could result in team members overextending themselves and burning out. Team member roles should be allowed to ebb and flow and change over time as the work of the group changes.

As a team chooses goals and activities, the team should take into consideration federal and state regulations, initiatives, and activities. This provides the team with the opportunity to be both proactive in both its responses to potential new mandates and understanding and predicting the implications of these mandates on various programs and activities. An example of this is the increased emphasis in the United States on standards and outcomes for young children. The development of standards and outcomes can provide communities with a unique opportunity to support more positive transitions across programs by working together to ensure that standards and outcomes are cohesive and complimentary across age spans and programs.

Choosing and implementing goals and activities that are responsive and proactive to both local needs and state and federal requirements and initiatives require attention to the operation of the team and the level of participation of team members. The operation and participation of the team members fall into three basic levels: active participant, resources, and key stakeholders. The level of involvement of particular team members often depends on the following:

- The ability of a team member to commit the time needed for team meetings and work associated with transition planning. Considering how transition activities fit into the person's job responsibilities in the agency can be helpful.

- The specific focus of the activities under development by the team, their potential impact on the person's agency and program, and the person's knowledge and expertise in the areas addressed

- The level of authority needed by the team during the decision-making and development process and how the person fits within the hierarchical needs of the activity. For example, if policies are going to be recommended, an administrator who understands and affects policy may be preferred to a teacher who primarily implements policy.

As team members determine the level of participation of various participants, the worksheet in Figure 4.2—completed here for the Metroville interagency transition team—provides a format for recording the decisions of the team. This form can be used to list specific positions and names of stakeholders according to their level of involvement and to outline key roles of these participants as identified by the team. A blank copy of this form is provided on page 173 in the appendix.

Active Participants

The majority of the work done by the team will be accomplished by a small group of active participants who meet on a regular basis as part of the community planning process. Most people agree that it is best to limit the number of active team members to between five and nine regular participants (e.g., Francis & Young, 1992). This allows for multiple perspectives but also helps keep the group efficient and on task. At this level, team members should commit at least 1 year to the team, which supports continuity in the planning and implementation process.

Determining Team Roles	
Level of involvement	**Key roles**
Active participants (core team of 5–9 members): Claire—Director, Metroville Head Start program Sue—Preschool Coordinator, Metroville public school system John—Healthy Start Coordinator, Metroville Health Department Mary—Director, First Steps Early Intervention Program Barbara—Director, Child Development Centers of Metroville Mike—Council Chair, Metroville Success by Six	Meet monthly to develop and implement annual community transition plan. Provide recommendations to agencies on needed changes in policies and procedures. Provide information as needed to agency and community groups on transition activities being implemented.
Resources (assist with information sharing and so forth as needed): University faculty Teachers and providers	Provide input into specific activities on community transition plan as needed. Serve on small workgroups to develop specific materials based on transition plan.
Key stakeholders (those who need to be kept informed and from whom support is needed): June—Assistant Superintendent, Metroville School Lucy—Chair, Local Interagency Council Brenda —Chair, Head Start Advisory Board	Provide final approval of community transition plan and take specific recommendations forward as needed for higher level approval.

Figure 4.2.   Determining team roles. Sample: Metroville, USA.

Generally, teams meet on a monthly basis during the initial stages of the community transition system development process. The frequency of meetings decreases as teams become more effective and more familiar with the community planning process. As the active team members work through these decisions, they should keep in mind that they have primary responsibility for assessing the concerns of the community related to transition planning; developing the long-term goals and short-term objectives and outcomes; and providing support and oversight for the implementation process.

Two additional questions also need to be addressed. These questions address the specific authority of the team and team members to make decisions about transition activities. Addressing these issues early on in the process will help ensure that the team is able to produce outcomes and products that will be supported by the community and the represented agencies.

What authority will the transition team members have to make decisions about the transition practices, policies and procedures, and activities chosen and implemented? How will this authority be established and formalized? The team will only be able to produce positive outcomes if it has the authority needed to make decisions about transition activities that will occur on both an interagency and intra-agency basis. Therefore, team members must work to establish this authority. This may include outlining the specific steps and processes they will need to go through to get final approval for specific actions and activities. Specific lines of authority will vary from team to team depending on the agencies involved in the transition-planning process, the specific structure of each agency, and the status and structure in place to support interagency collaboration within the community. For example, in one community, the team may be officially designated as the community-level transition team. This team may then forward key recommendations to a local interagency council in the county for final approval and support. In another county, the transition team may serve as the local interagency council, and final recommendations may be presented to each agency for final approval and support on an individual basis.

What steps will be taken to determine the extent to which team members are authorized to participate in and make decisions that affect their agencies (e.g., budget, staff time)? The authority of the transition team potentially may be affected by the specific authority given to individual team members. Therefore, at the individual level, team members must secure authorization for making decisions that will affect their specific agency or program. This requires individual team members to work with their supervisors and others in their individual agencies to determine the level and extent of their authority to make decisions that will affect their agencies. Once the specifics of his or her authorization are finalized, each team member should provide information to the team about what types of decisions he or she is authorized to make and when he or she will need to get additional approval from higher authorities in his or her agency. Individual team members tend to have different authority levels based on their particular agency structure. For example, in a small agency, a director of a program may determine that the individual participating on the team has the authority to make all decisions, both programmatic and financial. In a larger agency, the team member may be able to make programmatic decisions but may need approval from a higher level of administration for financial obligations.

Resources

In addition to active team members, resource personnel can be identified and engaged as appropriate to help the team address specific issues. For example, if the team determined that a major activity would be working on collaborative implementation of Child Find activities, then it may be appropriate to include the coordinator of Child Find services for early intervention and/or preschool as a part of a short-term workgroup or as a guest for a particular meeting. The key role of resource personnel is to provide information and support to the team in accomplishing a particular task or activity.

Key Stakeholders

Although the active members of the team do most of the day-to-day work involved in accomplishing the goals and outcomes, other key stakeholders within the community need to be kept informed of the group's work and provide needed support in implementation of new activities, policies, and procedures. An example may be the superintendent of a public school or the executive director of a local program. In general, key stakeholders do not attend regular meetings, although they may be invited periodically to meetings that involve annual planning and/or updates.

SETTING THE STRUCTURE: MEETING STANDARDS AND PRACTICES

Much of the work of the transition team will be done in meetings. Although many early childhood professionals spend a lot of time in meetings, few have had the opportunity to learn about specific strategies that can be used to help make meeting time more effective and efficient. Most learning about meetings comes from experience—trial by fire. A number of strategies and meeting processes—defining roles, using meeting agendas and planning, defining the meeting environment, and so forth—can be used by the transition team to help move the team through the stages of development and accomplish the vision of the group.

• • •

As Bonita was getting ready to leave her office for the transition meeting, the telephone rang. She glanced at her watch to see how much time she had. Should she answer the telephone? "Oh well," she thought. "They never start on time anyway, and when I get there they will just have to rehash what they have done and catch me up to speed. They do that for Melanie all the time anyway." She answered the telephone.

• • •

Each team establishes its own culture or way of operating. Many times, this culture is established unconsciously by the group in the first few meetings. This culture dictates how the group will operate, how members will be treated, and what happens to team members who "break the rules." For example, Bonita's team in the previous vignette has a ground rule that includes starting and ending meetings on time; however, Bonita knows that there will be little consequence if she is late to the meeting. The group will revisit what has happened so far, enabling her to get caught up on what she missed. Allowing a particular team member to disregard the ground rules established by the team without specific consequences can hurt the ability of the team to reach its goals. In the case of Bonita, because a ground rule about being late has been established by the team, the team should refrain from revisiting the work of the group when Bonita arrives late. This puts the responsibility for catching up with the group on Bonita and not on the group.

Defining Roles and Leadership

As described earlier, successful teams are able to accomplish their goals when team members actively participate. One key to ensuring active involvement of team members is to give each team member his or her own clearly defined role and responsibilities; team members will more likely actively participate on a regular basis when they have a specific role to fill. Therefore, one of the first steps in the team process is to determine the leadership structure of the group—what roles are needed and who will fill those roles. Several roles are critical to the group's successful development and accomplishment of their vision. They include the following:

- *Chairperson:* The chairperson of the group can be seen as the long-range planner, communicator, organizer, taskmaster, and evaluator. The primary responsibility of the chairperson is to make sure that the work of the group gets done and the group stays focused on the tasks at hand.

- *Recorder:* The recorder is responsible for ensuring that the work of the group is documented using a group-recording process, known as group memory (discussed later in the chapter), that is determined by the group. The recorder also maintains the records for the group and is responsible for making sure forms and minutes are brought to the meetings and disseminated to members in a timely manner.

- *Timekeeper:* Much of the work of the group will be done during meetings, and a timekeeper can help keep the group on task and focused. Specific strategies for setting time limits are provided in the section on agenda building on page 57.

- *Contact person:* Depending on the size and focus of the group, appointing a contact person for the team is sometimes helpful. The contact person can answer questions about the group's activities and vision and represent the group in other meetings and activities, as appropriate. For example, this person might be responsible for representing the transition team in other interagency meetings such as the Interagency Coordinating Council.

- *Gatekeeper:* The gatekeeper is responsible for helping the team use the structure and ground rules selected to accomplish the work of the group. The gatekeeper can help remind the team of processes to be used to make decisions, initiate discussions as to whether the ground rules are or are not being followed, and help keep the group on task by reminding them of items that are coming up on the agenda or by establishing a "parking lot" for items that need to be discussed but that are not on the agenda for the current meeting.

The team should determine additional roles and responsibilities based on the team activities and the structure that the team designs to accomplish its work. Whatever roles are deemed appropriate, the team should take time to determine how often roles will change and to outline the specific responsibilities for each role. Many times, team members agree to fulfill specific roles for a set period of time—usually a year or for the duration of the annual action plan. At the end of that year and when new activities and goals are selected, roles and responsibilities can shift as well. The key is to spread the work across members so that no one team member is overburdened. Team members can use or modify the Determining Responsibilities worksheet provided in Figure 4.3 to document team member roles, terms, and key responsibilities. (See page 174 in the appendix for the blank photocopiable form.)

Determining Responsibilities		
Role	**Term**	**Responsibility**
Chairperson: Claire	July 2006–June 2007	Facilitate monthly meetings, prepare agenda
Recorder 1: John **Recorder 2:** Barbara	Recorder 1: July–December 2006 Recorder 2: January–June 2007	Record proceedings on flipchart paper during meetings, transcribe and e-mail to team
Gatekeeper: Mike	July 2006–June 2007	Ensure ground rules are posted at each meeting, update as needed, keep group on track
Timekeeper: Maria	July 2006–June 2007	Track time during meeting as indicated on agenda
Contact person: Sue	July 2006–June 2007	Respond to questions about transition team activities by members of the general community as needed
Other: Community Council Liaison—Mary	July 2006–June 2007	Participate in community council meetings, provide updates of transition team activities and initiatives

Figure 4.3. Determining responsibilities (sample).

Using Meeting Agendas and Planning

The agenda for the meeting sets the tone and is a key indicator of whether the meeting will be successful. The agenda tells the participants what to expect and what preparations they need to make. A well-constructed and organized agenda can help demonstrate the preparedness and effectiveness of the team.

Two things to consider when putting together the agenda are the content and the process. The content refers to the specific items to be covered by the group. The content of the meeting is determined by the team, preferably at the end of the previous meeting, and is documented in the minutes by the team recorder. The recorder then prepares hard copies of the next meeting's agenda and provides them to the other team members as part of the minutes. This allows team members to participate in the meeting-setting process and also allows members to plan for upcoming meetings. Establishing a regular format for meetings can help facilitate the agenda-building process. This allows for continuity across meetings and—like setting the next meeting's agenda at the current meeting—helps participants better prepare for meetings. For example, standing agenda items could include beginning the meeting with a welcome and introductions followed by a quick overview of the agenda with options for additional input and last-minute topics for discussion or actions and ending the meeting with next steps and assignments. A sample agenda, completed for the Metroville interagency transition team, is provided in Figure 4.4 (see page 168 in the appendix for the blank, photocopiable form).

The processes used during a meeting also are critical to the team's success. Process refers to how meeting content will be covered and includes the specific meeting strategies that will be used by the team to accomplish the day's activities (e.g., group discussion, brainstorming). The meeting processes are generally determined and proposed by the chairperson or facilitator and reviewed as part of the meeting opening. The chairperson or facilitator may want to review the agenda made by the recorder prior to its distribution; that way, the strategies that will be used to accomplish the activities on the agenda also can be placed on the agenda to help facilitate the operation of the upcoming meeting. The chairperson or facilitator of the group also is responsible for gathering the materials necessary for the process agenda that has been developed (e.g., flip chart paper, index cards, handouts, markers/tape, refreshments) and bringing these materials to the meeting.

Defining the Meeting Environment

The environment where the meeting takes place is also important to consider because the room setup and location can greatly enhance or disrupt the meet-

	Process Agenda		
Topic/time allotted	**Action/process**	**Materials**	**Facilitator/ discussant**
Welcome/ introductions	Review roles and responsibilities; post meeting ground rules, vision, and current action plans on walls.	Name tags	Claire Sue
Agenda and process overview	Present agenda and process to be used; revise as appropriate.	Topical agenda on flip chart Paper copies of process agenda	Claire
Letter of intent	Present/discuss purpose, desired outcomes; group discusses key components to include. Determine working group and develop timelines for action.		Sue and John
Developing staff and family transition needs assessment	Present/discuss purpose, desired outcomes; group discusses key components to include. Break into two working groups (family and staff). Each group develops specific recommendations about specific process for gathering information. Group uses flip charts to record recommendations. Present to large group for discussion and decisions. Develop next steps, action plan, and timelines.	Flip chart, pens	Claire
Next steps/ agenda building	Review decisions and assignments made during this meeting. Determine agenda, time, and location of next meeting. Adjourn.		Claire

Figure 4.4. Setting a process agenda. Sample: Metroville, USA.

ing process. When planning meeting rooms and locations, the team should consider the following:

- *Access:* The meeting space should be accessible to all team members. Depending on the needs of the team, consider rotating locations so that people have a chance to visit each other's programs and/or agencies. Also keep in mind, however, that having meetings in a central and consistent location may reduce travel time and the time necessary to disseminate logistics and directions.

- *Visibility:* All team members should be able to participate in meaningful dialogue; therefore, the meeting table should be set up to allow team members to see each other without straining to look around obstacles and other people. Generally, round or rectangular tables work best; this allows each member to see the face of every other member of the group.

- *Sufficient work space:* The team will spend a large portion of their time together in action-oriented planning and discussions, so each team member should have sufficient work space. Team members also should have space to post work for other members to see and enough space for the team to be able to divide into smaller workgroups.

- *Minimize distractions:* The meeting space should be chosen with care to minimize outside distractions, including noise and disruptions from outside the meeting. As part of this process, team members should discuss if meeting in a team member's building or agency will pose a distraction to the team. For instance, for some team members, their own staff may feel free to interrupt a meeting with routine questions and/or concerns. This would be a distraction to the team.

STRATEGIES TO SUPPORT EFFECTIVE DISCUSSIONS

For most people, the majority of meeting time is spent in discussion and dialogue. However, nothing is more frustrating than discussions that go around and around and lead nowhere. A number of strategies, such as setting discussion guidelines, setting meeting guidelines and ground rules, using brainstorming, determining a process for recording group memory, and setting decision-making rules can be used by the team to help ensure that discussions are productive and result in action by the team.

Discussion Guidelines

One strategy for facilitating high-quality discussions is to develop a set process that will be followed during all team discussions, both large group and small group. For example, a discussion format that has been found to be successful for some teams includes the following:

- *Present:* Present the topic for discussion to ensure that all members understand what is going to be discussed. Post the topic for discussion on flip chart paper or an overhead projector to help keep the group focused.

- *Review:* Review past activities related to the topic at hand. This can be in handout format or a quick review of where the team has been and what decisions have been made.

- *Discuss:* Discuss the topic. If people stray from the topic, use the visual reminder to help refocus, and record stray topics for later discussion.

- *Decide:* Make decisions about next steps. This can include tabling the topic until more information can be gathered or making a decision about steps or strategies to be taken by the team.

Meeting Guidelines and Ground Rules

In addition, meeting guidelines and ground rules that are determined by the team can be posted during team meetings and used to help the team focus. Examples of rules that would help to facilitate high-quality discussions are as follows:

- Come to meetings with the necessary materials based on the agenda for that day. If team members do their homework and/or read the minutes in advance, meeting time can be better spent and the meeting itself can be more effective.

- Listen to each other. Preoccupation and disruptions lead to ineffective decisions by the group.

- Make an effort to be actively involved in group discussions.

- Respect the differing opinions and points of view of fellow members. Lack of diversity causes teams to become static in their activities.

- Present different ideas or points of view in constructive ways to broaden the discussion and allow for more creative solutions and strategies.

- Refrain from arguing about information that can be verified with a telephone call or by looking up the answer. This wastes valuable time.

Sample meeting rules for Hobart County are presented in Figure 4.5.

Brainstorming

Brainstorming is a process that can be used to limit actual discussion time so that a large number of potential items can be generated in a short amount of time. Therefore, brainstorming can be used to enhance discussion by getting many ideas on the table at once and then using a filtering process to eliminate

---

Meeting Rules

Start on time.

Begin with introductions and a clarification of the roles (e.g., chair).

Provide an overview of the agenda for the meeting.

Set time limits for each area of discussion, if applicable.

Discuss all topics on the agenda using the following steps for each topic:

    1. Present the topic for discussion.

    2. Review past activities related to the topic.

    3. Discuss the topic.

    4. Make decisions.

Review all decisions made during the meeting.

State the next steps the team needs to take, including the following:

    1. Set topics and date for the next meeting.

    2. Develop the agenda.

    3. Set the time and location.

End on time.

Figure 4.5. Meeting rules. Sample: Hobart County, USA. (*Note:* If roles are to change every meeting, new roles should be decided at the end of the meeting.)

all ideas but those that have the highest potential for success. When done well, brainstorming allows for the generation of a lot of information in a short amount of time. The team should consider establishing a process for when and how brainstorming should be used by the group and should develop a set of steps to be used by the team during a brainstorming session. Figure 4.6 provides sample steps that have been successfully used by transition teams. These steps include narrowing and defining the topic of discussion, setting a predetermined length of time for discussion, selecting a recorder and timekeeper, and after the brainstorming session ends, clarifying ideas, and making decisions based on ideas that are feasible. The team benefits from developing rules or

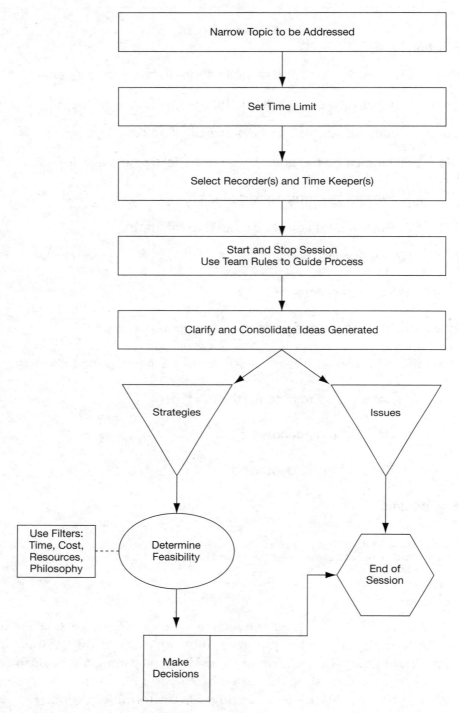

Figure 4.6. The brainstorming process.

guidelines for brainstorming sessions prior to the actual session. Examples of brainstorming rules include the following:

- Criticism of generated ideas is not allowed.

- All ideas should be encouraged and built on during the session.

- The object of a session is quantity not quality; remember that time will be taken later to look at feasibility.

- The team continues until the timekeeper calls time. Some of the best ideas are generated toward the end of a session.

Recording Group Memory

The transition team should have a process to record the group's memory of decisions and actions taken by the team. Therefore, the techniques used to record group work also can greatly enhance both team meetings and follow-up. The general process for recording meetings is the use of meeting minutes. Although minutes provide a record of what happened, they are generally written by one member of the group, the recorder, and are thus representative of the recorder's perceptions of what happened and what was said during the meeting. In a typical meeting, these notes are disseminated either after the meeting or at the next meeting, at which time participants are asked to make revisions or approve the minutes.

For the transition team, a group-recording process is recommended. Group recording refers to a process in which the work of the group is posted around the room using chart paper or butcher paper, index cards, and so forth. The group shares in the process of recording the decisions and actions of the group. As a result, minutes from meetings reflect only that information that the group agrees on in advance—if it isn't recorded on the wall and approved, it doesn't make it into the minutes. Several advantages for using group-recording processes include the following:

- Group decisions are displayed immediately.

- Off-task discussions are minimized by keeping the group visually focused on the topic of discussion.

- Team consensus is reached easily because all options are readily viewed and available.

- Group-recording notes can be used for later minutes so that one person is not writing instead of participating.

- Group progress toward a goal can be evaluated easily because the work is displayed and available.

Some group-recording strategies can be used to help the team adopt and effectively use group recording:

- Summarize points of discussions from the group so that all members can see. It is not important to capture everything that is said—only the main points.

- Check with the speakers to verify content. Once something is written, the speaker is responsible for making sure the information was captured correctly.

- Use bullets or color to denote changes in topics. This will help the team evaluate and record the discussion process. For example, the topic could be written at the top of the paper in green; the potential strategies, issues, or points of discussion in blue; final decisions in red; and next steps in purple. At the end of the meeting, the team will be able to quickly scan the wall to see what decisions have been made and to pull off items for a to-do list.

- Number the charts so they may be transcribed into minutes after the meeting. This will save time and energy on the part of the recorder.

Once the meeting is over, the proceedings from the meeting should be typed and disseminated to the group. The team can make decisions on how minutes should be organized and disseminated, including the timeframe for when minutes should go out to the group. Some teams find it helpful to include a list of who attended the meeting. Other teams also include lists of "key decisions" and "things to do" with the minutes on different-color paper to make it easier for people to catch up and follow up after the meeting. Finally, including the date, time, location of the next meeting, and the agenda that was generated by the team with the minutes is important.

Using the meeting strategies presented in this chapter can help ensure that the planning and implementation process of team meetings will have a major impact on the development of the transition system. Figure 4.7 is an organizational tool that can be used to determine meeting components and strategies to be used during team meetings. (See page 175 in the appendix for the blank, photocopiable form.)

Team Meeting Structure	
Meeting component	**Strategies or components**
What general meeting guidelines will the group follow?	Follow group meeting rules as established. Meeting rules are revisited annually or as needed based on monthly meeting evaluations. All meetings will start and end on time. All meetings end with generation of next agenda.
How will the group address meeting logistics such as regular meeting time, dates, and locations?	Core Team meets 2nd Tuesday of every month, 8:30 A.M.–11:30 A.M., large conference room, Metro Public Library, 4th Street.
How will the leadership issues of the group be addressed, including leadership structure (e.g., facilitator, recorder), leadership election, rotation schedule, and role clarification?	Rotation of leadership by vote occurs annually. General roles are outlined in Determining Responsibilities worksheet and include chairperson, recorder 1 and 2, gatekeeper, timekeeper, contact person, and community council liaison. A person may continue in a specific role for 1 additional year only. Mentorship is provided by those who previously held a role.
What are the group's rules for brainstorming?	All ideas are encouraged; no negative verbal or nonverbal communication is permitted. Go for quantity not quality. Build on others' ideas.
What are the group's rules for discussion?	Come prepared for planned discussions. One person at a time may speak. Show respect for and listen to other points of view. Provide potential solutions for problems and issues. Actively participate in discussions.
What group recording process will be used by the group?	Using flip chart, record major topics in blue, discussion points in green, and decisions in red. Minutes of meetings come from flip chart notes. Minutes are distributed within 1 week of meeting. Minutes include major decision and to-do lists. Minutes are distributed by e-mail.
What opportunities will be provided for participants to get to know each other as individuals? (Building of people-to-people relationships can have a major positive impact on interagency relationships.)	Longer meetings will be held in June and December and will include lunch. All meetings will begin with 5 minutes of latest news and events.

Figure 4.7. Structuring the meeting (sample).

SUMMARY

In this chapter, the authors provide a number of strategies that can be used by a local community transition team to develop and formalize an interagency structure that will help the team accomplish their goals and objectives. For many transition teams that have used this model, the interagency structure has proven to be one of the most critical components of the transition system's development process. When a team begins to lack direction or finds that they are losing the ability to be productive and make progress, returning to this chapter and revisiting these strategies will be helpful.

Chapter 5

Group Decision Making

The Hobart County transition team was just starting their monthly meeting. Janice was listening to Jill review the minutes of the last meeting. Jill reported that the team members had decided to hold a community screening on May 16. This is not at all what Janice remembered from their last meeting. She remembered that May 16 was proposed, but she didn't remember the team voting on that day or coming to consensus.

• • •

It is not uncommon for different team members to have different priorities, expectations, and recollections of events as they start the hard work of planning and implementing quality transition practices at the community level. Many people have experienced times when their perceptions of the decisions that have been made in a group meeting differ from those of colleagues. The transition team can avoid many problems by spending time at the beginning of the community planning process determining and formalizing how the team will make decisions and solve problems that may arise as part of the planning and implementation of transition activities.

TEAM'S ROLE IN DECISION MAKING

Both research and current practices in the area of education and early childhood, as well as other fields such as business, have recognized the critical nature of teams in defining and providing services and supports. In addition, research provides insights into the need for teams to solve problems and use effective decision making (Hollenbeck, Ilgen, LePine, Colquitt, & Hedlund, 1998).

Making decisions about the transition activities and supports to be implemented within and across agencies is a major task for the community transition team. As mentioned in Chapter 4, the team should end every discussion with a decision on the action to be taken by the team. These decisions are then recorded as part of the minutes for the meeting.

Teams can make decisions about the type of transition activity or strategy to be implemented in a number of ways. Depending on the team, some decision-making techniques will be more effective than others; therefore, the team should determine the decision-making techniques that will be implemented most often by the team and when and how these techniques will be used. The team also should come to consensus on the types of decision-making techniques that will *not* be used by the team. This information, once discussed, should be recorded on the worksheet provided on page 176 in the appendix (see Figure 5.1).

Decision Making		
Decision-making technique	When the method will be used (Type of activity or action)	How the decision will be documented
Default	1. When a decision cannot be immediately reached 2. When no options seem appropriate	1. Minutes reflect need for additional discussion or information. 2. Vote recorded in minutes along with rationale for vote.
Authority	Meeting agenda order and process	Written document (agenda)
Majority	1. Meeting logistics (e.g., time, location) 2. Roles and responsibilities 3. Choosing priority goals/outcomes	1. Record vote in minutes 2. Ballot (e-mail accepted) 3. Dotting on flip chart (minutes)
Consensus	1. Selection of specific strategies and practices implemented to meet goals/outcomes 2. Determining group ground rules	1. Meeting minutes 2. Meeting minutes
Clique	This method will not be used by the group.	
Other:		

Figure 5.1.   Making decisions (sample).

Default Decisions

Default decisions are used when the number of options from which to choose is limited. Default decisions fall into two types. The first type includes a situation in which only one decision is the right decision. This can be the result of finances, resources, personnel, or other factors. For example, a team identifies several strategies for providing cross-program training on new transition policies being implemented in the community. During the brainstorming process, team members identify three possible solutions: 1) find funding to pay for substitutes to allow all of the teachers to attend during the day, 2) break the training into three 1½-hour sessions that will occur from 6:00 to 7:30 at night, and 3) develop an on-line self-directed course to provide the training to staff. Due to the financial limitations within the community, options 1 and 3 clearly are not feasible at this time. Therefore, the default decision is option 2.

The second type of default decision is for the team to make no decision at all. This may be appropriate based on specific circumstances that make deciding on a course of action inappropriate or impossible at the time. This may include times when team members believe they do not have all of the information necessary to make a decision. In Hobart County, the transition team members identified the use of different curricula in programs across the community as one of the current barriers to a successful transition from preschool to kindergarten. Therefore, the team has been working to identify a standard curriculum that can be used across all preschool programs in the community. After careful review of the available curricular tools and the individual needs of each program, the team determines that nothing is currently available on the market that will meet their needs. Therefore, the final decision is to take no action at all. Default decisions usually are documented through meeting minutes that indicate 1) why other options were not feasible or 2) why the team felt a decision could not be made.

Authority Decisions

At times, the team may benefit from delegating specific decisions to a person or people on the team who serve in leadership roles. This means that the chosen person can make a decision and take action without the consent of the group. This type of decision is especially helpful when decisions do not require the full commitment of all team members to be effective or successful. Examples of authority decisions include the following:

- A **chairperson** or **facilitator** of a group may be given the authority to speak on behalf of the team to other groups, such as presenting the team's activities to a local interagency council or work group.

- The **facilitator** of a group may be given the authority to develop a process and plan activities to accomplish agenda items at a meeting.

- The **recorder** of the group may be given the authority to use funds to mail minutes of meetings, up to a set limit.

Once the team has determined who will be given specific authority to make decisions on behalf of the team, the types of decisions, by role, should be documented. The use of authority decisions can be documented as part of the group ground rules or orientation materials (as discussed in Chapter 4) or within the minutes of the meeting.

Majority Decisions

Majority decisions are the most commonly used decision technique and are generally arrived at through the use of a voting process. When determining when to use majority decisions, teams should carefully consider the potential implications of a majority vote. Use of majority decisions can be helpful when the team is struggling between two or more potential solutions; however, these decisions may not be appropriate if the team needs commitment and buy-in from all team members for the action to be successful. For example, using a majority decision may be appropriate when determining dates for upcoming meetings or because getting a date that will work for all team members may be difficult; using a majority vote to identify a specific transition practice for implementation across all programs may not appropriate.

With a majority decision, methods for documenting decision can include both verbal and written votes. The choice between these two types of votes should depend on the type of permanent record the team wants to have of the vote. A verbal vote can be recorded in the minutes, whereas ballots from a paper vote can be kept as documentation of the vote, with only the outcome being recorded in the minutes. A paper or e-mail voting process also can be used outside of a meeting when an immediate decision is needed by the group.

Consensus

Consensus decisions are made after the team has fully discussed all possible alternatives and the team as a whole believes that the course of action is appropriate. Consensus decisions are not those that indicate full agreement by the team but are those with which the team agrees to go along and support the decisions made. This type of decision-making technique is the most appropriate when all team members need to be committed to the action or activity that is to be implemented. For example, if the team is determining a specific action or policy that will need to be implemented by all members of the team to be successful, reaching consensus on a course of action will lead to higher levels of commitment from team members during implementation than will a majority decision.

Like other decision techniques, formal methods for reaching consensus need to be determined and followed by the team. The transition team can formalize the consensus process in a number of ways, such as the use of color cards or the thumbs up/down or fist five method. Each of these methods is described in Table 5.1.

Clique Decisions

At times, a few powerful individuals on the team make decisions about the activities implemented by the team. These individuals, sometimes referred to as power brokers, are individuals who have met aside from the group to design a course of action and to try to impose their views on the remaining team members. This type of decision making is not recommended for the transition team. A conscious decision by the transition team not to allow clique decisions can go a long way toward limiting this type of action. Documentation to not use clique decisions can be included in the meeting minutes or through the interagency structure (discussed in Chapter 4).

Table 5.1. Methods for reaching consensus.

Method	When it is used	How it is used
Color card or tents	During discussions to gauge the level of consensus in the group	During discussion, team members indicate their level of comfort with where discussions are headed by holding up their color card or turning their tent to the appropriate color: Red: I am having a problem with where we are headed. Yellow: I have some concerns about where we are headed. Green: I am okay with where we are headed.
Thumbs up/down	Toward the end of a discussion when the team is ready to move toward a decision	During discussion, team members indicate their level of comfort with where discussions are headed by holding up their thumbs: Thumb up: I am okay with the decision. Thumb to side: I have some concerns about the decision. Thumb down: I have a problem with the decision.
Fist five	Toward the end of a discussion when the team is ready to move toward a decision	When the group is ready to make a decision, the chair or facilitator can call for a fist five: Five fingers: I'm for it and will work hard for it. Four fingers: I'm for it, will work hard, and have a reservation or two. Three fingers: I'm for it, have serious reservations, yet will go along with it. Two fingers: I don't like it, won't work for it, but won't work against it. One finger: I don't like it, won't work for it, and probably won't work against it, but I'm not sure. Fist: I'll actively work against it; I cannot support it as it stands. If team members hold up four to five fingers, the group can move forward with the decision. Zero to three fingers mean more discussion is needed.

Meeting Evaluation

You know you have had an effective meeting if you can agree with the following statements.

YES NO

☑   ☐   The ideas and talents of the council members have been well used.

☐   ☑   The time spent arriving at decisions was well used.

☑   ☐   The decisions made are correct or high in quality.

☑   ☐   The decisions made will be acted on by all individuals in the group.

☐   ☑   The decision-making ability of the group has been improved.

Figure 5.2. Evaluation decisions (sample).

Because team members and the relationships among team members may change over time, the team should consider regularly evaluating the decision-making processes used by the team so that changes can be made as needed. For example, the team may review the decision-making techniques they have been using and determine that they never really used a particular strategy or that a strategy they have been using has evolved slightly over time. Using a formal process to review decision-making strategies and to evaluate the functioning of the team can provide important information that can be used to modify the approaches and strategies used. Figure 5.2 provides an example of an evaluation form that can be used to review the team's decision-making strategies. A blank, photocopiable form is available on page 177 in the appendix.

SETTING PRIORITIES

As the team makes decisions about the activities and strategies they will implement to address the transition barriers identified by the team, a process for prioritizing activities will become important as well. Given that transition is one small part of the job responsibilities of many agency staff, the team will have to make difficult decisions about which activities will take precedence to take advantage of team members' limited time and resources. Two strategies that have been used successfully by transition teams to prioritize their activities are dotting and voting.

When using dotting to prioritize activities, each team member is given a set of dots or markers of different colors. The number of dots provided depends on the number of items that need to be prioritized. Usually, three to four dots of different colors are sufficient. Each color dot represents a priority level and, optionally, a point value, as presented in Table 5.2.

Table 5.2.　Dotting to prioritize activities

Color	Priority level	Point value
Red	1st	4
Blue	2nd	3
Green	3rd	2
Yellow	4th	1

Team members are asked to place a dot beside each of their priority areas. Once all team members have placed their dots, the totals are calculated for each item and then ranked. If there is a tie in point value, team members can choose to rank them based on the color of dots. For example, according to the dot values in Table 5.2, if one item has two red dots, one blue dot, and one yellow dot for a total of 12 points, and another item has three blue dots, one green dot, and one yellow dot for a total of 12 points, the item with the highest priority dots (red) would be ranked higher than the other item.

Voting is another method that can be used to prioritize. In voting, a simple majority of votes (or tally marks) for an item would indicate its ranking. This process can be completed by allowing all team members to have one vote or a number of votes (three to four), dependent on the number of items to be ranked. Specific rules for the voting process should be discussed with the group prior to voting. For example, it should be decided if team members must spread their votes across items or if they can put all of their votes on a single item. Team members can use the worksheet on page 178 in the appendix (see Figure 5.3 for a sample) to document their decisions related to which priority-setting methods they plan to use. The worksheet allows the team to document when they would use a particular method. For example, the team may use dotting

Setting Priorities		
Method	**To be used for**	**Process to be used**
Dotting	Decisions that will require full commitment of the team for successful implementation Determining activities or practices for implementation	Four dots or colors Red—4 points Blue—3 points Yellow—2 points Green—1 point Ties in points broken by those with the largest number of high-value dots (e.g., red over blue, yellow over green)
Voting	Decisions about general functioning of the group such as agenda, time and location of meetings, and so forth Choosing specific strategies for implementing a specific transition practice or strategy that has been selected by the team	One vote each for all member agencies (even if more than one representative attends a meeting) Raising of hands during face to face meetings to indicate vote Use of tallies on flipchart to determine specific items to implement Use of e-mail voting for items needing immediate attention between face-to-face meetings
Other		

Figure 5.3.　Setting priorities (sample).

when they want to determine action or activities that will require full commitment from the team and when the action has a direct impact on services for children and families. They may elect to use voting for more general actions of the team related to their team functioning, such as when and where to hold meetings. For each method, the team should outline the specific process they would use to implement the method (e.g., the steps in the process to be used).

COMPLAINT RESOLUTION AND PROBLEM SOLVING

Conflict is a natural part of the team process for any group. In fact, to not have some sort of conflict in a team is rare. Lack of conflict in groups actually can inhibit the creativity and successful movement of the group toward their vision (Amason, Thompson, Hochwarter, & Harrison, 1995; Berstene, 2004; Hopen, 2004). Effective teams are able to head off serious and long-term problems in the team by both understanding indicators of conflict in a group and establishing procedures for how to deal with conflict when it arises. As demonstrated in Figure 5.4, conflict generally arises out of unmet basic human needs, including sense of belonging, power, freedom, and fun. These basic needs also are combined with limited resources in agencies and potentially different values among the members of the team. Generally, three responses to conflict include avoidance, confrontation, and communication, only one of which leads to resolution. By using and understanding the sources of, indicators of, and responses to conflict, the team stands a better chance of both understanding and responding appropriately to conflict in the group when it occurs.

The following is an example of how the conflict pattern illustrated in Figure 5.4 can occur.

• • •

In the small community of Hobart County, all of the members of the transition team need to have their basic needs met as part of their participation. Some basic needs are stronger than others. Sue has a strong personal need for a sense of belonging. Sue was unable to attend the last interagency transition team meeting because her youngest child was home sick. At the meeting, the team decided to devote a full meeting in September to outlining procedures for transition conferences based on the Individuals with Disabilities Education Improvement Act of 2004 (PL 108-446). When Sue found out about the actions of the group, she was upset for two reasons. First, an important decision was made while she was not in attendance (thus not meeting Sue's basic need for a sense of belonging). Second, she really felt that the group needed to finish their work regarding Child Find before moving on to the transition conferences (different priorities), which she thought she had made clear before the last meeting.

• • •

SOURCES OF CONFLICT

Limited Resources
- Time
- Money
- Assets

Unmet Basic Needs
- Need to feel a sense of belonging within the group
- Need to have power or control over decisions and actions
- Need to have the freedom to make decisions and take action
- Need to have fun and feel good about your involvement.

Different Values
- Convictions
- Priorities
- Principles

CONFLICT

Indicators of Conflict

Intensified Feelings
Hardened Positions
Dehumanization
Punishment
Deterioration in Communication

RESPONSES TO CONFLICT

Avoidance

Team Members who:
- do not attend meetings
- do not talk during meetings
- do not follow through

Confrontation

Team Members who:
- threaten to leave the group
- raise their voices during meetings
- talk about the group to others outside the group

Communication

Team Members who:
- ask for clarification
- make it a point to try to understand other points of view
- bring in outside facilitators when needed

Unresolved Conflict

Resolved Conflict

Figure 5.4. Sources of and responses to conflict.

Sue's strong need to belong as well as her priority differences resulted in potential conflict with her fellow team members. As teams develop their action plans and make decisions about transition processes, individual members often signal—through some basic actions—when their needs are not being met or when they feel conflicted because of limited resources or differences in values from their fellow team members. Indicators of conflict generally start with intensified feelings, resulting in members of the team passionately stating their cases or becoming withdrawn from the group. These indicators can escalate to the point that communication between team members deteriorates and falls apart.

Sue may demonstrate several indicators of conflict that may be visible to the facilitator or other members of the group. First, Sue may contact the chair of the team with intensified feelings about the group's decision. If this does not result in a change or an explanation with which Sue feels comfortable, she may advance along the continuum of indicators illustrated in Figure 5.4 and refuse to participate in the September meeting unless she gets her way or drop out of the group altogether.

To help manage conflict in the group in a constructive way, transition team members should be aware of indicators that individuals are feeling un-

---

The Hobart County team will utilize the following process and strategies for complaints and conflict resolution and problem solving for issues encountered during the transition system development process.

Complaints

All community and transition team members have the right to address issues and concerns with the planning process at regularly scheduled meeting times. When possible, areas of concern should be briefly discussed with the current facilitator and placed on the next meeting's agenda for discussion. If the complainant and the facilitator feel it necessary, a special meeting can be called to discuss the issues and concerns.

The team will refrain from participating in and airing complaints when not in the presence of other team members at a regularly scheduled or specially called meeting.

Conflict resolution and problem solving

The Hobart County transition team strives to create an atmosphere in which conflicts and problems are addressed openly and effectively. The team agrees that through conflict they should improve their relationship of mutual trust and respect of team members.

Process to be used for complaints, conflict resolution, and problem solving
The team will
1. Clarify current perceptions from all parties as to the focus of the conflict or problem
2. Discuss the conflict as it relates to the shared vision and needs of the team and community
3. Discuss past conflicts and the strategies employed to address the conflict
4. Generate options for addressing the conflict
5. Develop a specific action plan if necessary to address the conflict
6. Formalize the resolution and plan

If a resolution cannot be reached by the team, an outside facilitator or mediator will be contacted.

Figure 5.5. Conflict-resolution and problem-solving procedures for Hobart County.

comfortable by staying attuned to fellow members' verbal and body language. Using the consensus-building strategies presented earlier in this chapter also can help reduce conflict and/or at least give team members the opportunity to voice their opinions before the conflict escalates.

One key strategy for addressing potential conflicts in the transition team is to establish a formal process for conflict resolution and problem solving. This allows the team an opportunity to talk through potential conflicts and have a written process in place that team members can refer back to when and if problems arise.

A sample of conflict-resolution and problem-solving procedures for Hobart County is presented in Figure 5.5. In this example, the team has addressed two key components during their design of the formal conflict-resolution and problem-solving process. First, the group started with an introductory paragraph that provided information about the overall intent of the procedures as they relate to complaint, conflicts, and problem solving. Second, the team outlined in detail the steps that will be taken to address issues brought forth by team members or identified by the chair of the team. By formalizing the process for complaint and conflict resolution, the team was able to articulate agreement among team members for the process prior to any conflict occurring, take into consideration typical conflict patterns (as presented in Figure 5.4) and help ensure that if conflict does occur, the group can move directly toward resolution.

SUMMARY

This chapter focuses on providing examples and strategies for helping the local interagency transition team determine methods and procedures for group decision making and for addressing potential conflict in the group. Both of these components of the team planning process help set a foundation on which good decisions can be made that move the group forward in addressing transition issues and concerns that arise in the community.

Chapter **6**

Barriers to and Assessment of Current Practices

Juan has been with the Hobart County Early Intervention program for many years. As a regional coordinator, he has long been concerned about the transition of his students into the public preschool program. Over the years, Juan has read many articles and documents about the importance of quality transition planning, but every year at least one family, child, or provider approaches him with a new problem or issue for him to address. Some of the problems he has addressed before, but every year brings something a little different.

• • •

Janice has been providing services in Metroville for many years as the preschool coordinator for the school system. Over the years, she feels that she has developed close working relationships with many early childhood agency staff members. However, she just cannot seem to make any progress with the Head Start program. She is concerned that their lack of communication and collaboration is having a negative effect on the transition of young children into the kindergarten program.

• • •

Once the transition team has established a vision for transition and an interagency structure and determined how the group will make decisions, the focus of the team can turn to identifying the specific issues and barriers to

Table 6.1.   Commonly reported barriers to a good transition to preschool and kindergarten

Work required in the summer is not supported by salary.
A transition plan is not available.
Visiting homes is dangerous.
Parents do not bring their child in for registration or open house.

effective transitions in the community and assessing the needs related to communication, collaboration, and the current status of transition practices.

IDENTIFYING CURRENT BARRIERS TO A GOOD TRANSITION

Numerous barriers to a quality transition have been identified, as discussed in Chapter 2. These include commonly reported barriers to a successful transition to kindergarten (Pianta, Cox, et al., 1999) and to preschool (Rous, McCormick, & Hallam, 2006). Although some commonalities do exist among these barriers, as listed in Table 6.1, the community should identify specific barriers based on the community demographics and economics and service system, as discussed in Chapter 3. The following process is helpful in identifying community barriers to the transition process.

Step 1: Each team member is given a stack of Post-It notes or index cards. Team members work individually to identify specific issues or barriers to effective transitions in the community. Team members should write one issue or barrier per Post-It note or card. The goal is to generate as many issues and barriers as possible in 5–10 minutes.

Step 2: As a team, discuss and consolidate similar issues. For example, one team member may have written "Preschool teachers do not get information about incoming students in a timely fashion," another team member may have written "We do not get information on incoming kindergarten students," and yet another member may have indicated that "teachers do not share information about their students." The team may determine that these barriers are similar and can be consolidated into one barrier—"Information about children transitioning into new programs is not shared."

Step 3: Once issues have been consolidated, a final list of issues should be developed (see Table 6.2). The team should keep this list of issues and barriers because the team will refer to them later as they identify specific activities they want to address and develop a plan for implementing these activities.

Table 6.2.   Transition barriers identified for Hobart County

Little or no communication exists between teachers across programs and agencies.
The curriculum has little consistency across agencies.
Families get different and sometimes erroneous information about programs their child might be attending after the transition.
Hobart County has no written transition policies or procedures.
Agencies use very different referral forms, and families must submit the same information multiple times.
No one person is in charge of the transition process in many agencies.

ASSESSING THE CURRENT STATUS OF COMMUNICATION AND TRANSITION ACTIVITIES

Individual members of the transition team can assess the current status of communication, collaboration, and transition activities between their program or agency and other agencies represented on the transition team. Team members can assess the current status of these items from an individual agency standpoint and from a community standpoint. For example, individual members of the team can assess their current level of collaboration with the other key stakeholders on the transition team (as identified through the process discussed in Chapter 3). They also should assess the level to which transition activities have been integrated at a community level.

Communication Across Key Agencies

Communication across agencies and programs is a key factor to the success of building a community transition process. Good communication includes understanding the nature of communication strategies used between agencies, the comfort level of individual team members in communicating with other agencies, and individual team members' familiarity with other agency's programs and practices. Individual team members can use the worksheet on page 179 in the appendix (see Figure 6.1 for a sample) as a way to assess the current status of communication and then identify strategies for strengthening the communication among agencies. To complete the assessment, individual agency representatives rate the degree to which they agree with a series of statements describing communication practices. After individuals have completed the assessment, they may choose whether to share the information with their team members. Reassessing the status of communication on an annual basis can help individual agencies and the team document improvement in communication channels.

Transition Activities

Two steps can be followed to assess the current status of transition activities.

Step 1: Determine the types of activities that are in place within individual agencies and the degree to which these activities can be identified as standard practice. Standard practice indicates that the activities are in place across classrooms or providers in the agency. For example, one common practice is that "staff implement strategies to support needed skills in the post-transition environment." This practice supports the notion that the identification and assessment of children's entry-level skills might facilitate their adjustment to the next environment—a blank, photocopiable form of which is provided on pages 180–181 in the appendix—Figure 6.2 provides a format that can be used to assess the current practices. Detailed information about the specific practices included on the form is provided in Chapters 7 and 8.

Analyzing Interagency Communication

Agency: Hobart Head Start   **Date completed:** 9/1/06

1 = strongly agree, 2 = somewhat agree, 3 = somewhat disagree, 4 = strongly disagree

	Early intervention	Public school— preschool	Public school— school age	Head Start	Child care
We use primarily formal communication strategies (e.g., written) with this agency.	1 ②3 4	1 2 3 4	1 2 ③4	1 2 3 4	①2 3 4
Contacting this agency is easy when I have questions or need to get in touch with them.	①2 3 4	1 2 3 4	1 2 ③4	1 2 3 4	①2 3 4
I am in contact with this agency on a regular basis as part of my work.	1 ②3 4	1 2 3 4	1 2 3 ④	1 2 3 4	①2 3 4
We have been able to work with this agency to solve common issues and address problems.	1 ②3 4	1 2 3 4	1 2 ③4	1 2 3 4	①2 3 4
The staff members in this agency are responsive to my requests for information and assistance.	①2 3 4	1 2 3 4	1 ②3 4	1 2 3 4	①2 3 4
I am familiar with terminology used by this agency.	1 ②3 4	1 2 3 4	1 2 ③4	1 2 3 4	1 2 ③4
I am familiar with the specific transition activities regularly implemented by this agency.	1 ②3 4	1 2 3 4	1 2 ③4	1 2 3 4	1 ②3 4

Figure 6.1. Analyzing interagency communication (sample).

Assessing Status of Transition Activities

Use the following chart to assess the current status of transition practices and activities in individual agencies. Indicate the status of each practice by placing a ✓ in the appropriate column. If a practice is in place (partially or as a standard practice) indicate how that practice is supported in your agency. If you don't know, leave the column blank.

Transition practice or activity	Individual agency status				Practice is supported through		
	Not in place	Partially in place	Standard practice[1]	Don't know	Written procedure or agreement	Technical or written guidance	Nothing in writing
1. Staff have key information about agencies and services available in the community.		✓					✓
2. A single contact person for transition is identified from each agency.	✓						
3. Broad-based transition activities and timelines are identified (e.g., open house, Child Find).		✓					✓
4. Processes are in place for child- and family-based transition meetings.			✓		✓		

[1]Standard practice means that all staff in your agency or program regularly implement the activity or practice.

Figure 6.2. Assessing status of transition activities (sample).

Step 2: Determine the extent to which standard transition practices are in place across agencies and programs. Figure 6.3 is a sample of a worksheet that can help team members identify where standard practices exist (see page 179 in the appendix for the photocopiable worksheet). Information from the individual assessments (Figure 6.2) is consolidated to provide a picture of which practices are in place in which agencies and where gaps exist in practices within the community.

SUMMARY

Transition planning at a community level requires a great deal of communication and collaboration across agencies and programs. It also requires that the community team have a clear handle on the barriers that are affecting the transition process and the current practices and activities that are in place across agencies to support better transition experience for children and families.

The remaining chapters in this book provide specific information and guidance on how transition teams can identify strategies and practices that can be used to help address the barriers identified by the team.

Chapter 7

Program Practices

Programs engage in numerous practices that support the transition process for young children and families, such as updating community resource information, formalizing interagency procedures across agencies, and coordinating and participating in community transition events. These practices generally are guided and supported by administrative functions and often are implemented by staff who work directly with children and families. Transition-planning practices are most effective when implemented on a collaborative basis across agencies and programs, using the processes described in earlier chapters. This collaboration increases continuity in transition planning across the early years (Rous, Hallam, Harbin, McCormick, & Jung, in press) This chapter presents the way in which collaboration among agencies can positively affect specific program practices related to administrative and staff functions.

ASSUMING RESPONSIBILITY FOR THE TRANSITION PROCESS

One of the keys to successful transition planning is identifying those individuals who have responsibility for overseeing specific transition activities in an agency and for communicating with other agencies. Transition services for the families of Maria and Marcus (see the following vignettes and Chapter 8) were improved by the ability of multiple agencies to contact each other and plan for transition opportunities such as cross-program visitation and family meetings.

● ● ●

Marcus Thomas has been identified as having language and motor delays and is receiving services from the state early intervention system. Marcus' parents, Sarah and Joe, are both employed; Sarah works part-time as a secretary, and Joe works full-time as a mechanic. Marcus attends a family child care program 3 days each week while his mother works.

Marcus did not walk at the same age as his sister, and his parents were concerned about this but felt that he would catch up in a few months. When he still was not walking at 15 months, their family child care provider, Susan, shared her concerns with Sarah and Joe. They knew it was time to seek help. Susan gave them the number of the state early intervention system, and Marcus began receiving both speech and physical therapy services once a week.

The speech-language pathologist and physical therapist come to Susan's home where they work with Marcus and Susan. Once a month, the therapists come at the end of the day so that Sarah and Joe can participate with Susan in the sessions. The Thomas family and Susan are both committed to ensuring that Marcus receives optimal care and education. They feel that the therapies are making a big difference in Marcus' development.

As Marcus approaches 3 years of age, the Thomas family has started talking with their early intervention service coordinator about Marcus's transition to preschool services. Their service coordinator, Jennifer, has shared information with them about the upcoming transition. Jennifer has let them know that preschool special education services are typically offered in the public school or Head Start program in their school district with therapies being provided in the classroom. Although Sarah and Joe are excited about the prospect of preschool, they are concerned that Marcus is too young to attend an elementary school with older children. They also really appreciate their therapists at the clinic and are very concerned about moving therapy services to the schools. All in all, the Thomas family is very apprehensive about the upcoming transition. Jennifer knows that Sarah and Joe are very concerned about Marcus's services, and she also knows that these parents want the best possible services for him. Jennifer arranges for the Thomas family to visit the two public preschool classrooms and the local Head Start site. Jennifer is part of a local interagency team that coordinates services for young children and their families in three rural counties. She knows the preschool coordinators for both the public school and the Head Start program and feels comfortable setting up the program visits.

● ● ●

Maria Jackson is a preschooler who attends a full-day Head Start program in her neighborhood. Maria lives with her mother, Juanita, and her grandparents in an apartment close to the Head Start program and her church. Maria began attending the Head Start program in the fall. During the summer, Maria and her mother relocated to Metroville so that they could live with family while Juanita attends a nursing program at a local community college. Maria has had some difficulty adjusting to the new environment. It has been hard for her to get used to her mother's long hours in nursing school. However, Maria loves her preschool program and she especially loves her teacher, Mrs. Martino. Mrs. Martino has visited her home and always talks to Maria's grandparents when they pick her up from school.

As spring approaches, the Jackson family realizes that they must prepare for Maria's transition to the public school. They are very excited about kindergarten but also are apprehensive about leaving the Head Start program. The move to a new city and a new neighborhood has been difficult for Maria, but she has become very comfortable with the Head Start program. Juanita is concerned that the transition to school will be difficult for her. Juanita knows that Mrs. Martino has made extra effort to get to know Maria and her family to help ease the transition. She has also benefited from working with the Head Start family service worker, who helped her in obtaining health benefits for Maria. Juanita wasn't sure what to expect from the public schools.

Mrs. Martino talked with the Jackson family about the transition to kindergarten. She had a class meeting for family members interested in preparing for the transition to school. She invited a few kindergarten teachers from the local elementary school, and they provided information about kindergarten programming and the information that families would need to enroll their child. They also talked about the kindergarten open houses that would be held right before school starts.

. . .

Facilitating effective transitions for young children and families requires both sending and receiving agencies to have efficient communication and information-sharing processes in place. On a practical level, knowing whom to contact to initiate these collaborative processes can streamline individualized transition planning and save time and energy for families engaged in the transition process. Because multiple agencies are involved in the transition process and individual agencies are responsible for referring families and children to other agencies, providing a resource to help ensure that agency personnel have information about other agencies and available services in the community is an important part of transition planning.

> The "Agency Information" section might be helpful in a community if the interagency transition team identified the following barriers to successful transitions:
>
> • One agency doesn't know who to call in another agency.
>
> • Program staff have a general lack of knowledge regarding community resources.
>
> • Families with whom an agency works are unaware of how to gain access to resources.

Agency Information

Optimally, each agency or service into or out of which a child may be transitioned will have its own transition team. When a child is referred for different or additional services, the transition team that is transferring a child to a new program will meet to determine the best way to inform the new agency or service about the upcoming transition. To know whom to contact in another agency, the transition team needs to collect and effectively use information about the various programs and agencies in a community.

In collecting agency information, an agency or program's transition team should have a primary goal to ensure that accurate information is presented, updated, and made useful to children and families in the program. Formalizing this information-gathering process will ensure that the transition team will be able to utilize current community resource information as they work with families in the transition planning process. The following list outlines specific steps and considerations that can guide the process of collecting agency information. A sample letter requesting agency information is provided in Figure 7.1.

Specific Steps and Considerations for Collecting Agency Information

1. Identify basic information about each new agency that provides services for children and families so that providers and families can identify the most appropriate program or setting for the child. Relevant information includes the following:

    • Services provided

    • How eligibility is determined (the federal and state mandates followed)

November 22, 2006

Dear service provider:

Our Hobart County interagency transition team is working through a process designed to facilitate the transition of children from birth to 5 years of age as they move among early childhood programs in our county. A part of our plan is to put together a resource manual that includes information about all of the services and supports available in the community. Teachers and other direct service providers will use this information as they plan for a child's transition.

You can help our efforts by sending us the information below so we know who to contact in your organization as we go forward to smooth the transition process in Hobart County.

Sincerely,
Hobart County transition team

Please mail the bottom portion of this form in the enclosed stamped envelope or fax it to Mary at 888-555-1357 by December 6, 2006.

- -

Agency name:

Address:

Telephone number:

Fax number:

Ages of children served:

A brief description of your services/program:

Contact person for your agency:_____
                                                              (Name)

                                       _____
                                                              (Title)

Telephone: _____ E-mail: _____
                  (Number)   (Extension)

Figure 7.1.   Letter requesting agency information (sample).

- Funding for the agency and fees charged to consumers

- The population served by the agency

- The agency philosophy

2. Determine the best mechanism for formalizing and sharing the information collected in the first step with the program staff (e.g., web-based resource directory, written directory), and take into consideration current documents the agency may have that can be refined or updated.

3. Determine which staff members need access to the information.

4. Determine a process for updating information about the agencies on a regular basis.

5. Develop and recommend agency policies, procedures, or guidelines that address how the transition resource materials will be used in the agency to facilitate transitions.

6. Provide information and/or training to staff about the resource directory or other materials and expectations for their use.

●　●　●

In Hobart County, the interagency transition team used the contact information gathered by the individual agencies participating on the team to develop a community-wide resource guide. The purpose of this guide was to assist service providers and the transition team in identifying and gaining access to service information across community programs. As part of the maintenance of the resource guide, the Hobart interagency transition team sends out annual surveys to local agencies so that they can revise the community guide and provide staff with the most current agency information.

●　●　●

Contact Information

Each agency should have a single contact person who is responsible for coordinating the transition process for young children and their families. The contact person should be identified by title, not name, because individuals commonly change jobs and positions. Other key pieces of information that agency staff should have are the hierarchy and channels of communication in each agency. For example, within a public school system, an early intervention provider needs to know when to contact the district office as opposed to contacting the school directly as well as who within the school is the most appropriate contact person (e.g., principal, guidance counselor, teacher) depending on the purpose of the communication. If a teacher is unavailable, who is the next person in the hierarchy to contact?

Specific Steps and Considerations for Acquiring Contact Information

1. Determine which person in a specific agency whom staff, families, and administrators should contact for information and/or support regarding transition activities.

2. Gather information on the specific heirarchy and channels of communication within each agency.

3. Develop and recommend agency policies, procedures, or guidelines that address how the contact information will be used in the agency to facilitate the transition.

4. Provide information and/or training to staff about the contact and communication information and expectations for its use.

CRITICAL STEPS IN DEFINING INTERAGENCY TRANSITION PROCESSES

A number of critical steps can help to smooth the transition process for administrators, staff, families, and children. These steps involve the delineation of an infrastructure for transition planning in an agency by outlining broad-based transition activities and a transition timeline. Generally, these steps will address the specific regulations that provide direction to agencies and programs such as Head Start, early intervention, and public preschool special education. However, these activities also support the successful transition for all young children as they move among various programs.

Identifying Broad-Based Transition Activities and Timelines

Most agencies provide a number of supports to children and families as they make the transition into and out of their agencies or programs. To better facilitate these activities on a community level, it is helpful for the interagency transition team to discuss the types of transition activities that each agency supports and when these activities occur. This allows the team to identify the types of activities that are being implemented across programs and to examine areas of duplication that may allow for potential consolidation or collaboration to make better use of resources. For example, both Head Start and a public school may conduct community screenings during the same month in the

Milestone	A	S	O	N	D	J	F	M	A	M	J	J	Responsibility
Schedule staffing meetings.		X	X	X		X			X	X			Prescreening committee
Conduct observations.		X	X	X	X	X	X	X	X	X			Preschool chairperson, preschool representative
Schedule the IEP meeting.					Ongoing								Preschool chairperson
Send evaluations and cumulative records to kindergarten teachers.										X			Preschool chairperson
Attend monthly transition meetings.	X	X	X	X	X	X	X	X	X		X	X	Transition team
Initiate new referrals.					Ongoing								Infant/toddler and preschool program teachers
Work with family resource centers.	X	X	X	X	X	X			X	X	X	X	Preschool chairperson, preschool representative
Organize parent orientation.		X											Preschool chairperson; infant/toddler, preschool, and kindergarten representatives
Conduct parent orientation.			X										Preschool chairperson, preschool representative, family resource director
Begin mid-year transition checklist.				X									Teachers
Begin receiving program observations and evaluations.				X									Teachers, preschool chairperson, preschool representative
Complete mid-year transition checklist.							X						Teachers
Plan staff in-service training.					X	X							Preschool chairperson, preschool representative
Conduct staff in-service training.						X							Scheduled presenters
Plan open house for families.						X							Kindergarten and preschool coordinator, preschool chairperson, teacher representative
Conduct cross program visitations.								X					Kindergarten coordinator, infant/toddler representative, preschool chairperson

Figure 7.2. Timeline for transition milestones (sample). (*Note:* The letters A, S, O, N, D, J, F, M, A, M, J, and J correspond to the months in a year beginning with August.)

spring to identify children who may be eligible for their programs. By consolidating these two activities, parents and children could participate in and receive information about both events at the same time. In addition, the Head Start and public school programs could participate in joint public relations activities such as creating parent orientation information and planning meetings and program visitations, thus reducing costs. Figure 7.2 presents a sample timeline for transition milestones. Timelines can provide the framework for planning of transition events. Target dates, such as fall enrollment in preschool or spring Child Find activities, provide a means for agencies to plan more efficiently and effectively together.

Specific Steps and Considerations for Identifying Broad-Based Transition Activities and Timelines

1. Identify the current transition activities that are being implemented in each agency and the timeframe for these activities.

2. Identify areas of potential collaboration and consolidation of activities.

3. Determine a formal mechanism for sharing information about community-wide activities and events (e.g., community transition calendar).

● ● ●

In Metroville, the transition task force identified several agency activities that occur in their community, including spring family transition meetings and staff transition training. The transition task force determined that these activities could be much more effective if they were planned and implemented across agencies rather than having single agency transition events. In Maria's situation, the jointly planned Head Start and public school kindergarten transition meetings for families allowed Juanita to gain much-needed information about preparing for kindergarten in a timely fashion.

● ● ●

Transition Practices that Require Administrative Attention

A number of practices require the attention of the transition team at the administrative level. Such practices generally revolve around identifying children for appropriate services and maintaining communication between agencies and staff in order to follow up with the child and family after the transition process.

■ The "Identifying Broad-Based Transition Activities and Timelines" section might be helpful in your community if the interagency transition team identified the following barriers to successful transitions:

- Teachers are not prepared for children who are making a transition to their program.

- Families are not prepared for the change to a new program and/or a new philosophy.

- Regulations/rules across programs are challenging and affect the transition process.

- Children are not receiving timely services.

- Critical members of the child's team are not showing up for important transition meetings.

- A lack of congruency exists across programs in transition activities.

- Children are tested too much.

- Confidentiality issues among agencies are a problem.

- Information is duplicated on forms.

- People are saying that transition "is not my job."

Transition Meetings Transition meetings are an opportunity for families to become acquainted with new services and staff and to support families and children as they prepare for changes in programs and/or services. Two specific types of transition meetings are group and individual. Group transition meetings, such as orientations and meet-and-greets, provide opportunities for families to meet other families and agency representatives, learn about new programs, and discuss specific services and supports.

Individual transition meetings provide an opportunity for families to prepare for the transition process by learning about their specific options for services, meeting with specific program representatives from the programs in which they might be receiving services, and developing a plan to prepare for the transition. Programs such as early intervention (funded through the Individuals with Disabilities Education Improvement Act of 2004, PL 108-446,

Part C) and Head Start require staff to hold transition meetings or conferences with individual families as part of their transition services. Other agencies do not have specific requirements for transition meetings but conduct meetings as part of their transition services or are asked to attend meetings hosted by other agencies and programs.

Questions to Consider When Planning for Transition Meetings

1. What type of transition meetings—individual and/or group—are currently in place in the community?

2. For group transition meetings

    *   Can events be coordinated to take advantage of the expertise and re-sources available in the community?

    *   What responsibilities do direct services staff and other professional staff have during transition meetings and events?

3. For individual transition meetings

    *   What current requirements and practices are used during these meetings?

    *   Who should participate in individual transition meetings across agencies?

    *   Which service providers and community members should be invited, and what methods will work better for invitations (e.g., written contact, telephone call)?

    *   Can transition meetings be scheduled at specific times to increase the likelihood that representatives from all agencies can attend? Do specific months work better than others? Days of the week? Times of the day?

    *   When should meeting invitations go out?

    *   Will families be involved in constructing the meeting agenda and invitation list? If so, in what ways?

    *   What forms are agency staff members responsible for completing? Who sets up the meetings? Who schedules the meetings?

    *   What are the family's roles and responsibilities during the transition meetings, and who works with them to help them understand this process?

Enrollment and Referral All programs have a process for how children and families become enrolled in their programs. Some programs use informal processes, some use application processes, and others use more formal and regulated referral processes. For families who are enrolled in multiple programs at the same time, or even over time, the enrollment process can be duplicative and cumbersome. For example, families often are asked to provide medical and developmental information about their child on every form for every agency. What can be done to reduce this duplication? Agency staff must become familiar with the individual requirements for each program to make appropriate referrals to the agency. The list of questions below will help guide administrators through this process to reduce duplication and increase their likelihood of success.

Specific Questions for Enrollment and Referral

1. Are there common forms or components of forms that can be used across agencies and programs to help prevent families and staff from having to provide the same information multiple times?

2. Are there ways that information can be shared across programs? This requires parent permission and attention to federal confidentiality requirements (e.g., Family Educational Rights and Privacy Act [FERPA] of 1974 [PL 93-380], Health Insurance Portability and Accountability Act [HIPAA] of 1996 [PL 104-191]) that address myriad guidelines regarding the sharing of information.

3. What responsibilities do direct services staff and other professional staff have related to the referral process? What forms are they responsible for completing? What training will be needed in order to complete forms and participate in the referral process in appropriate ways?

Screening and Evaluation High-quality early childhood programs generally provide some level of developmental screening and/or evaluation of a child, which provides critical information for instructional programming. Some programs use informal screening and assessment processes, whereas others use more formal and regulated eligibility and evaluation processes. When children are enrolled in multiple programs at the same time, or even over time, the evaluation process often is duplicative and can be stressful to both families and children. For example, children may be tested by the sending agency to gather exit data about the child's development and by the receiving program after transition to gather entry data about the child's development.

Specific Questions for Planning Screening and Evaluation

1. Are there screening, evaluation, and assessment tools that can be used across programs that have similar goals?

2. How can screening and evaluation information be shared among agencies that are serving the same children or that are receiving children into their programs while keeping with state and federal confidentiality requirements (e.g., FERPA, HIPAA)?

3. If a program needs to determine eligibility of a child prior to program entry, how can it take advantage of evaluation information already available from another program to prevent retesting or duplication of information?

4. What responsibilities do direct services staff and other professional staff have related to the evaluation process? What forms are they responsible for completing? What training will be needed in order to complete forms and participate effectively in the process?

• • •

In Maria's situation, the Head Start teacher received consent from Juanita to share assessment information with the public school. The Head Start teacher gathered both informal and formal assessment data and formally submitted the information to the public kindergarten in June prior to Maria's transition. The sharing of this information allowed Maria's kindergarten teacher to become familiar with her educational needs prior to enrollment. Specifically, Maria's teacher developed an understanding of Maria's strengths, needs, and unique characteristics that may influence individualized educational programming for her.

• • •

Follow-Up Activities   Follow-up activities provide a mechanism to examine the effectiveness of transition planning and procedures. The three levels of follow-up that can be helpful in providing information to strengthen and support transition activities and the supports in place after the transition are child, family, and program.

At the child level, it is important to gather information about the child's success in the next environment to determine whether the transition strategies and practices that were implemented were helpful for the child's adjustment to the new program. Child follow-up activities can take multiple forms, including site visits, parent reports, receiving staff reports, and other documentation that provides helpful information about the child's adjustment and success in the new environment. Sample follow-up procedures and a child summary form are included in Figures 7.3 and 7.4, respectively.

Follow-up with families about their satisfaction with the transition-planning efforts and the impact of these activities on the transition is critical. Interviews and surveys with families are two particularly helpful ways that families can provide feedback to agencies regarding their transition experiences. In addition, this can be a particularly effective way of obtaining recommendations for improvements in transition planning.

Determining the impact of transition efforts on the program's ability to provide quality transition services also is an important component of the follow-up process. This means determining the degree to which specific activities were implemented and that staff had the information they needed to actively participate in the activity. Asking for the staff members' opinions of how the transition process can be refined to better support children and families also is important. This type of programmatic evaluation can involve a review of program documents to examine staff records regarding steps taken in the transition process as well as conversations with agency staff regarding their perceptions of the effectiveness of the transition process.

Policy: Follow-up activities will be conducted that will facilitate a smooth transition and ensure program continuity.

Procedures:
1. During the year, teachers/staff will collect samples of each child's work.
2. From April to May, or prior to transition, the sending teachers/staff will assemble materials to be given in a follow-up packet to the receiving teachers/staff.
3. Items to be included in the packet include the following:
   • Child Summary Form (completed by the teacher who has worked most closely with the child) and cover letter to the receiving teacher
   • Samples of the child's work
   • Copy of the Transition Checklist, including end-of-year ratings
   • Assessment reports, particularly those recently completed that indicate the child's progress and current level of functioning
   • Copy of the most recent individualized family service plan/individualized education program, including transition objectives and progress noted
4. Follow-up packets will be sent to the receiving early childhood coordinator at the end of the school term or prior to the transition date by the director of each program.

Figure 7.3. Follow-up procedures (sample).

Child's name: Marcus

Date of birth: November 11, 2003

1. **Child's strengths:** Marcus follows directions well, is easily motivated, and loves animals. Marcus is very coordinated and a leader during outdoor play time. His preferences include water play and listening to stories on tape.

2. **Child's needs/suggested targets:** Marcus has limited verbal communication and delayed language, and he needs assistance communicating with his peers. Marcus does not like to be touched and has difficulty with self-help skills such as toileting and dressing.

3. This child learns best in these situations:

   ☒ small group   ☐ large group   ☐ one-to-one

   and by these means:

   ☐ visually   ☒ auditorily   ☐ tactilely

4. **Suggestions for classroom adaptations (e.g. seating, positioning, language):** Marcus does very well with picture cards to help with language. Sitting Marcus next to a verbal peer can help him model language. Using carpet squares or other indicators of space during circle time or other large group activities will help Marcus stay in his own space and address some tactile issues.

5. This child received the following support services:

   ☐ physical therapy   ☒ speech therapy   ☐ adaptive equipment

   ☒ accommodations (list):   ☐ other (list):

   picture cards and   _____

   communication board to   _____

   help with verbal language _____

6. **Specific behavior management techniques or supports/programs used with the child:** Physical redirection is not successful. Light touch to the shoulder, in combination with ensuring eye contact, is the most successful approach. Marcus loves animals, and animal stickers or time in the dramatic play area with the small animal toys (circus and zoo) work well for motivating him. Marcus is very peer oriented. Finding another child that he really likes and who can provide peer modeling has been very successful. A peer who is not overly affectionate (hugger) would be best given his tactile defensiveness.

Figure 7.4. Child summary form (sample).

Specific Questions for Follow-up Activities

1. What types of follow-up activities are currently in place across programs? Are they required as part of federal or state accountability and monitoring processes?

2. How can follow-up activities be coordinated so that information can be shared across programs and across time?

3. What specific roles and responsibilities do direct services staff have in follow-up activities with children and families?

4. How will follow-up data be collected and shared with staff, families, and children and in keeping with state and federal confidentiality requirements (e.g., FERPA, HIPAA)?

● ● ●

After Marcus made the transition from early intervention to preschool, his service co-ordinator contacted the family 30 and 60 days after the official transition to determine whether the family felt prepared for the transition experience and whether services were being received as originally planned.

● ● ●

The "Facilitating Implementation of Transition Activities by Staff" section might be helpful in your community if the interagency transition team identified the following barriers to successful transitions:

• Staff have a lack of understanding of individual roles in the transition process.

• Timelines are not being adhered to as required.

• Staff have a lack of understanding of interagency partner roles.

• Partners do not understand legal responsibilities or responsibilities of other agencies.

• Relevant information about the child is not shared with receiving programs.

• Relevant information about the child is not used by receiving programs.

Facilitating Implementation of Transition Activities by Staff

Once the specific procedures for transition activities have been negotiated and formalized at the administrative level with appropriate input from staff and families, the team develops specific mechanisms for outlining agency policies and procedures for staff members. This includes outlining procedures within each agency as well as the ways in which the procedures and practices are co-ordinated across agencies and programs. This allows each staff member to see the impact of his or her particular activities on other parts of the service delivery system. For example, the service coordinator for early intervention may be responsible for setting up the transition conference that occurs with the child and family prior to the age-3 transition. By understanding the local school district practices related to attendance at these meetings, the information other service coordinators will bring to these meetings, and the activities the school will implement to follow up after the transition conference, the service coordinator is better able to prepare the family for the experience. Outlining procedures for staff should be considered for transition meetings, enrollment and referral, screening and evaluation, and follow-up activities.

Specific Steps and Considerations for Implementing Transition Activities

1. Provide detailed descriptions of staff responsibilities in job descriptions, and include components of activities in job evaluation processes.

2. Provide staff training on staff responsibilities both on an intra-agency and interagency basis.

3. Provide copies of written guidance documents (e.g., regulations, policies, processes) with in-depth orientation for new staff and annual updates for existing staff.

● ● ●

As part of the Metroville kindergarten transition task force, the interagency group determined that the Head Start and public school programs needed to identify staff from each agency who would coordinate spring transition activities. The public school program selected their early childhood coordinator, whereas the Head Start program selected a family service worker. These staff work together to plan joint events for families and staff. They also serve as liaisons within their own agencies.

● ● ●

The administrative design of transition activities is an important component to effective transition practices. Transition activities that are devised from a community perspective and integrate important transition functions within the life of an agency help to promote ongoing, high-quality transition practices for young children and their families. The maintenance of these activities also is essential. The following section describes how to maintain staff and family involvement throughout the transition process.

The "Maintaing Staff and Family Involvement" section might be helpful in your community if the interagency transition team identified the following barriers to successful transitions:

- Staff demonstrate a lack of respect regarding a family's concerns about the transition process.

- Administrators do not get feedback from teachers.

- Families and staff do not have a significant role in transition planning; rather, they are told to just do it.

- Forms often are handed to families and staff without asking for family and staff input.

- Staff are not trained in how to complete forms.

- Staff and families have little communication about the transition process or activities that have been helpful.

Maintaining Staff and Family Involvement

The likelihood that transition processes will be successful in agencies and across the community is partially dependent on the involvement of staff and family members in the design of transition practices and activities. Both direct services staff and families have intimate contact with the child involved in the transition, and both have been integrally involved in planning and implementing transition activities. Maintaining their involvement throughout the development process not only is wise but also will go a long way toward ensuring success. Identifying both staff and family concerns and needs related to transition in a systematic way is helpful so that the transition team has input into what activities they should focus on.

Specific Steps and Considerations for Maintaining Staff and Family Involvement

1. Determine the best method for collaboratively assessing staff and family concerns and needs. This can happen through a number of venues (e.g., annual surveys, focus groups, group meetings, suggestion boxes).

2. Determine formal methods for staff and family input into transition activities and processes as they are being developed. Share forms and procedures with staff and family members to get their feedback prior to finalizing. In addition, once forms and processes have been developed, ask for feedback again once staff and family members have been using the forms or procedures and have information about their effectiveness and efficiency.

3. Provide staff and family members with information via staff newsletters, e-mails, and training/informational sessions about the activities of the transition team, what is being worked on, and how things are progressing.

4. Provide specific information to staff and families about how the transition activities and process are helping to support congruency among programs to better support the transition process.

In both the Hobart and Metroville communities, transition activities are posted in multiple locations to keep staff and families informed. Many agencies post the information on their web sites, display announcements at the agency offices, and include the information in their parent newsletters.

Staff Involvement in Transition Activities

For staff and administrators, one of the most proactive ways to support positive transition experiences for families and children is by providing quality early care and education services. Research about the benefits of quality early care and education cannot be ignored. Research has documented that high-quality early education results in higher academic outcomes for children (Magnuson, Meyers, & Ruhm, 2004; National Institute of Child Health and Human Development [NICHD], 2002; Ramey & Ramey, 2004). Ultimate success in school is one of the outcomes we hope to achieve as part of a successful transition process. Research has shown that children who receive quality care outperform their counterparts in academic areas, are more likely to attend college and hold jobs that require higher-level skills, and are less likely to be placed in special education classes (Olsen, 1999). Providing for a firm foundation of skills in the early years allows children to be more successful in any environment to which they will transition.

The importance of *classroom climate,* or the emotional context of the classroom, on student achievement also has been well documented. In fact, classroom climate has been linked to how students behave and feel about school, themselves, and others (e.g., Fraser & Fisher, 1986). Factors to consider when talking about classroom climate are communication patterns, norms about what appropriate behavior is and how things should be done, role relationships and role perception, patterns of influence and accommodation, and rewards and sanctions (Johnson, 1980; Johnson & Johnson, 1975; MacAulay, 1990). At the intra-agency level, programs can enhance the transition process by creating a caring community of learners and promoting a positive climate for learning. This can be achieved by attending to the specific instructional techniques used to facilitate learning and the environment in which these services are offered. Providing a climate of mutual respect allows for positive teacher-child interactions, including ensuring that staff provide motivation for learning and social skills development and use positive guidance in teaching skills (Bredekamp & Copple, 1997).

At the interagency level, the transition team can consider a number of specific classroom and programmatic practices as part of the transition system development process. These practices can facilitate a smoother transition for children and families as programs work to coordinate their instructional efforts as well as facilitate collaboration in the professional development of staff.

The "Continuity of Child Expectations and Curriculum" section might be helpful in your community if the interagency transition team identified the following barriers to successful transitions:

- The curriculum across programs does not mesh and the transition team is unable to see how one program connects with another.

- Providers get a general lack of respect across programs (e.g., early intervention, preschool, high school, kindergarten).

- Program staff involved in transition do not understand what happens in other programs.

CONTINUITY OF CHILD EXPECTATIONS AND CURRICULUM

Since the 1990s, an increasing emphasis has been on setting standards and expectations for what children should know and be able to do in the early years.

These standards and the specific curricula and teaching strategies used in programs to assist children in their growth and developmental processes are critical to laying the foundation for successful transitions. Therefore, transitions of children in communities in which children and families must adjust routinely to changes in expectations and curricular approaches can be difficult. In other words, if the expectations and teaching approaches for a child moving among various agencies and programs change with each move, the child will have difficulty making continuous progress.

At the program level, the transition team should support continuity across expectations and curriculum by working together to identify those expectations and curricular approaches being used across programs. This type of collaboration promotes shared expectations for child behavior and learning. This does not mean that programs must adopt the same curriculum but rather that programs must understand different curricular approaches and consider the potential connections among early childhood programs.

Specific Steps and Considerations for Providing Continuity of Child Expectations and Curriculum

1. Determine the degree to which programs are using child standards, outcomes, and/or expectations and the congruency of these expectations across programs in the community.

2. Identify the curricular approaches being used across programs, how these approaches are linked to the specific expectations for the child, and what assessment methods are being used to measure the child's progress.

3. Develop a process of showing linkages across expectations and curricular approaches between programs and agencies to help staff identify how their approach meshes and enhances approaches used by other programs' staff.

• • •

In Metroville, the kindergarten transition task force reviewed the curriculum at the preschool and kindergarten levels in an effort to facilitate children's transitions between these programs. Their review revealed that much variability existed at the preschool level across different types of preschool programs. This led to group discussions among the preschool directors and kindergarten staff. The focus of these discussions was to understand the curricular differences among the programs and come to consensus on some key curricular components that should be integrated across all programs to prepare children for kindergarten. As part of these discussions, the task force determined that facilitating social competence and developing social skills were important at the preschool level and that programs addressed this in many different ways. They then determined to work together to develop a social skills curriculum that could be used by various preschool programs.

● ● ●

The "Staff-to-Staff Communication" section might be helpful in your community if the interagency transition team identified the following barriers to successful transitions:

- The transition team does not feel that they have time for interagency activities, meetings, planning, and so forth.

- The transition team cannot share information with other programs because of confidentially requirements.

- Teachers do not understand how other programs work and what their focus is.

- Teachers/providers do not know what skills children need to be successful in the next environment.

Staff-to-Staff Communication

The heart of the transition process is centered in the ability of staff to communicate across programs and agencies; unfortunately, the work and teaching responsibilities of staff sometimes prohibit their ability to do this. A number of specific transition activities can support and enhance communication among staff members, such as joint training, program visitation, sharing of child-specific information, and interagency meetings.

Joint Training As community transition teams identify areas of need related to the transition process, staff-to-staff communication about expectations, procedures, and practices can be enhanced through the provision of joint training (Jang & Mangione, 1994; Rous, Hemmeter, & Schuster, 1999). Joint training is the creation of an opportunity for staff at sending and receiving agencies to engage in professional development activities together. Joint training efforts are helpful in promoting continuity of services, building relationships among staff, helping to define specific transition activities, and maximizing resources across programs and agencies. These training opportunities should be carefully planned so that they are in response to specific agency professional development needs, such as a early literacy development or assistive technology, as well as responsive to different agency capacities, such as financial and scheduling constraints (Swan & Morgan, 1993). As part of the training process, cross-agency peer coaching can be used to both support and assist in the implementation of new skills and knowledge. Peer coaching in this context would be staff-to-staff support across agencies on a particular element of program practice, such as designing classroom environments or facilitating parent meetings. Teams also should consider providing social situations in which staff from both programs can meet and discuss transition issues on a more informal basis.

Specific Steps and Considerations for Joint Training

1. Link training opportunities and determine training needs by reviewing staff needs and concerns on a regular basis.

2. Determine which concerns and needs have been identified across agencies and programs and can best be met through training on a joint basis. Some specific areas that are particularly suitable for joint training as it relates to the transition process include the following:

   - Regulations for agencies involved in the transition process

   - Receiving and sending agency purpose, eligibility requirements, operation, and funding (i.e., understanding what each individual agency does)

   - Strategies for helping young children and families understand program options

   - Staff involvement in due process (e.g., referral, evaluation, meetings)

   - Staff role in the transition process (i.e., getting the young children and family ready to transition)

3. Determine how often trainings need to occur. Consider how the information provided in the training will be provided to new staff and whether returning staff will need annual or regular updates.

4. Determine how joint training sessions will be funded.

5. Determine the best format for the training experience. For example, should written information be provided to support the implementation of new

skills and behaviors after the training event, and is this provided jointly or by individual agencies?

6. Provide regular meetings and sharing sessions across programs and agencies.

7. Identify the specific administrative support that staff will need, including providing mechanisms for and encouraging communication between teachers via telephone, e-mail, or other modes of communication.

● ● ●

In Hobart County, early intervention and preschool staff jointly plan a 1-day training each year to address common professional development needs related to transition practices. The county interagency group coordinates the training with needs assessment information from local agencies. Last year's training focused on involving families in the transition process and included effective communication strategies.

● ● ●

Program Visitation Providing opportunities for staff from one program to visit other programs and classrooms also enhances staff-to-staff communication. Program visitation can play a vital role in helping to build relationships, understanding, and knowledge across programs (Bredekamp & Copple, 1997; Howell, 1994; Meier & Schafran, 1999; Rous, Hemmeter, & Schuster, 1994). The knowledge gained and relationships forged during program visitation help staff follow up on children after the transition process and see the environments in which children will be participating to help prepare them for the transition.

Specific Steps and Considerations for Program Visitation

1. Develop a systematic method of cross-program visitation and schedule cross-program visitation for all staff members. For example, sending agency staff may visit receiving agency programs in the fall when programs have just started, and receiving agency staff may visit programs in the spring as children get closer to the transition point.

2. Develop the rationale and mechanisms to obtain support of supervisors in cross-program visitation, including mechanisms for securing release time for staff.

• • •

In Metroville, the kindergarten transition task force kicked off their transition efforts by having the kindergarten teachers visit the local preschool programs. This was the first time many of the kindergarten teachers had visited the preschool programs. The teachers reported that this was very helpful in understanding the children's transition experiences. The task force is planning to sponsor the preschool teachers' visit to the public school kindergarten programs next spring.

• • •

Sharing of Child-Specific Information   By the time a child leaves a specific program or service, the direct services staff working with that child have gained a vast amount of information about how to work with the child and his or her likes and dislikes, how to handle the child's difficult behaviors, and how to motivate the child. This information needs to go with a child to the next environment so that staff at the next agency, who are new to the child, do not have to start from the beginning. Providing formal mechanisms for sharing a child's information across programs can be instrumental in smoothing the child's adjustment to the new environment. One of the best ways to evaluate the effectiveness of the shared child-specific information is to follow up with children and families in their new environment to determine how successfully the transition to the new placement is going.

Specific Questions for Sharing Child-Specific Information

1. What type of information would be helpful for new teachers to have?

2. What format would work best for sharing the information?

3. What confidentiality issues does the team need to address?

4. What methods would work best for dissemination of the materials?

5. What role should family members play in putting together information and in the dissemination of information?

• • •

In Hobart County, the local interagency group determined that child evaluation and assessment information can be shared across programs as long as parental consent is obtained. In an effort to facilitate this information sharing, the local interagency transition group developed a shared confidentiality form that met all agency requirements. This form has become a helpful tool in the community. In Marcus's case, Marcus's parents signed the confidentiality form and then worked with their therapists to create a journal of Marcus's progress over the past year to be shared with his new preschool teacher.

● ● ●

Interagency Staff Meetings and Workgroups Some situations may occur during the transition process that require focused attention on a specific child or family or group of children and families. For example, a child with significant disabilities may be ready to make a transition from the Head Start program to the public school kindergarten program. Because of the child's intense needs, a more focused communication process may be helpful to support staff-to-staff communication during the transition process. The use of interagency staff meetings can provide the opportunity for agency staff to share information about specific children who may have more difficulty making the transition to a new program (Wheeler, Reetz, & Wheeler, 1993).

Specific Steps and Considerations for Interagency Staff Meetings and Workgroups

1. Develop a systematic process for determining situations for which individualized or small group staff-to-staff communication is needed. This includes helping staff know who to contact if they have a specific concern about a child or family or group of children or families.

2. Develop procedures for addressing confidentiality when information will be shared across programs and/or staff and for determining how meetings and outcomes will be documented and shared across programs.

3. Develop processes and procedures for how families will be informed and included in the process.

● ● ●

In both Hobart County and Metroville, the community interagency groups have developed communitywide policies on information sharing among agencies. These policies support effective communication among agencies and serve as the structure for individualized family transition conferences.

● ● ●

SUMMARY

The collaborative implementation of transition practices across programs and agencies increases the success of transition planning for young children and their families. Implementing specific strategies to support collaboration and communication among agencies for both staff and administrators is essential to an effective transition process. These strategies and practices revolve around critical points in transition for young children. Specifically, practices are outlined related to responsibility for the transition process and administrative support, critical steps in the transition process such as the enrollment process and supporting meaningful staff and family involvement, and practices that support continuity in child expectations and curriculum across programs and agencies. The program practices suggested in this chapter support effective transitions by helping community teams work through a process that includes the systematic gathering of information; development of cross-agency policies, procedures, and guidelines; and ongoing provision of training and professional development for staff in the implementation of transition practices selected by the community transition team.

Chapter 8

Child and Family Practices

The ultimate goal of community transition planning is to ensure the successful adjustment of children into new situations or settings and to ensure that the new experiences meet the needs of children and families. Transition experiences can be difficult for children, and supporting their positive adjustment to new situations should be a driving force in transition planning. Research has demonstrated that children can suffer academically as a result of little transition support (Entwisle & Alexander, 1998).

This chapter presents a variety of strategies and practices that support child and family preparation for and adjustment to new environments. The integration of child and family practices reminds transition team members of their pivotal role in facilitating effective transition experiences for young children.

CHILD PREPARATION

Preparing children for their next educational placement facilitates their adjustment and increases the likelihood of their success in the next environment (Entwisle & Alexander, 1998; Schulting, Malone, & Dodge, 2005). Children need and deserve information about and experience with the next environment so that they can feel more comfortable during the transition process.

• • •

Maria recently has experienced a variety of transitions in her home life—moving to a new neighborhood and living with her grandparents with her mother. Because of this, Juanita, Maria's mother, is concerned about Maria's success in the kindergarten program. In this scenario, information about Maria's family needs as well as her educational needs are important pieces of information to share with the professionals in the next environment.

• • •

Marcus, who lives in the Hobart community, faces another set of challenges as he and his family prepare to make a transition.

• • •

Marcus's transition involves changing programs, providers, and teachers as well as a change in his service delivery model (from home based to center based). Marcus's family has developed strong relationships with their early intervention service coordinator and therapists. Planning for Marcus's transition necessitates the involvement of many agencies because he receives early childhood special education services. Because Marcus has an identified disability, transition planning for him and his family must abide by the regulations set forth in the Individuals with Disabilities Education Improvement Act of 2004 (PL 108-446).

• • •

The most important elements of child preparation include sharing information between the sending and receiving agencies, developing an individualized transition plan, and paying attention to entry-level skills for preschool and primary-age children. Parents and professionals should work together when preparing a child for transition to make informed educational decisions.

Sharing Information Between Sending and Receiving Agencies

The development of agency policies and procedures to share child information appropriately is essential. Each agency should review agency and state guidelines regarding confidentiality to ensure compliance with these mandates (see Chapter 7). Once this is complete, agencies can develop procedures for sharing child information among programs and staff. These policies and procedures should outline the specific types of information to be shared, provide forms and guidelines for obtaining parental consent, provide information about contacts at other agencies, and discuss timelines for information sharing. These policies and procedures provide the framework for more substantive decisions focused on ensuring effective transition experiences for young children and families, such as locating additional required services or finding solutions to transportation concerns.

After procedures have been developed for information sharing, agencies can determine which information items should be included in children's records to be shared between the sending and receiving agencies. Although communities should develop their own list of specific child data to be shared among agencies, information typically consists of the following:

1. Introductory letter from sending to receiving agency

2. Program summaries, including child records

3. Copy of most recent program plan or individualized family service plan (IFSP)/individualized education program (IEP)

4. Copy of most current assessments

5. A portfolio—a child's work samples, anecdotal notes, and so forth—of child's learning and development

This list is a starting point for considering what should be included in a child's file to support his or her transition to the next program and/or environment. As communities focus on this area of transition planning, however, the information that is ultimately included should support the child and family's transition experience by ensuring that the receiving agency has all of the right information to proceed effectively. For example, up-to-date assessments provide teachers and other professionals with relevant information to plan for the child's entry into the new environment. A complete portfolio can provide in-depth information on a child's interests, dislikes, and the types of supports he or she may need to be successful in certain activities or environments.

Developing an Individualized Transition Plan

As communities establish the infrastructure for sharing information about individual children among agencies to ensure effective transitions, individualized transition plans should be developed for children preparing to move to a new learning environment. Individualized transition planning is a process that should be incorporated into the overall community transition plan. Through the community planning process, agencies should make decisions regarding the key elements that should be addressed as part of a child's transition plan.

Procedures for individualized transition planning for children should include examining specific child goals that will support a child's anticipated posttransition outcomes. Such outcomes could include a host of child skills that may support the child's participation and engagement in the next environment, such as social skills, dispositions toward learning, and/or self-help skills. Agencies working together can develop the methods by which individualized goals can be determined. Agencies can also determine appropriate methods of monitoring and evaluating transition goals and sharing this information with families and relevant agency staff. See Figure 8.1 for a sample Child, Family, or Community Transition Plan form. A blank, photocopiable form is available on page 182 in the appendix. Agencies can use additional pages as needed.

Child, Family, or Community Transition Plan

Date: _____   Community ☐   Program ☐   Family ☐   Child ☐

Family/child's name:_____

Child's date of birth:_____

Goal 1:_____

Indicator 1:_____

Indicator 2:_____

Indicator 3:_____

Steps/activities to support transition	Lead team member and others who need to be involved	Timeline	
		Date proposed	Date achieved

Figure 8.1. Child, family, or community transition plan (sample).

For children receiving early intervention or early childhood special education services, the inclusion of an individualized transition plan is a legal requirement. The Individuals with Disabilities Education Improvement Act of 2004 (PL 108-446) mandates that all children with disabilities have individualized transition plans and that families participate in a transition conference to plan for their child's transition. In transition planning for Marcus and his family, Marcus's individualized transition plan is integrated into his IFSP. Marcus's plan, as developed by the local professionals and his parents, is shown in Figure 8.2.

Paying Attention to Entry-Level Skills

A climate of educational accountability emphasizes the notion of school readiness and preparing children for school. This is particularly pertinent as one plans for a child's transition to kindergarten. It should be noted that most kindergarten teachers report social and self-help skills as particularly important

Child and Family Transition Plan			Date: 1/05
This plan addresses which of the following transitions? ☐ From hospital to home ☐ Between communities ☐ Service to a new setting ☐ Other: _____ ☑ Exit early intervention before 3ʳᵈ birthday ☐ Exit early intervention at 3ʳᵈ birthday			
Is this the official transition conference? ☑ yes ☐ no			
Our priorities or concerns related to this transition: Sarah and Joe would like Marcus to attend preschool after he turns 3. They are concerned about his transition to a group care environment, particularly his self-help skills at school.			
What we want to happen? Marcus and his family will be adequately prepared for the transition to preschool.			

Strategies or activities (include family involvement/exploration of options, agency discussion, child preparation and agency preparation and/or involvement	Target date	Date completed	People/agencies who will help and their role
1. Sarah and Joe will visit several preschool sites in the community.	10/05		Service coordinator will help to schedule these visits.
2. The school system will provide the family with information about the service referral process for different agencies.	3/05	3/05	Preschool coordinator will provide information.
3. Marcus will start attending a weekly library story hour to get him used to sitting in a group.	4/05		Sarah and Joe will take Marcus to story hour.

Family review (Date and initial)	No longer a need	Unsatisfied or worse	Unchanged; still a need	Partially met; still a need	Need met; satisfied	Comments:
						The service coordinator will continue to provide family with information and timelines for transition. The service coordinator will initiate the referral within 2 months. The IFSP team will locate videos and books on potty training that will help Sarah and Joe.

Referral activities (Date and initial)	Permission for records transfer	Records sent	Permission for referral	Referral initiated	
	3/05 BSR	3/05 BSR	3/05 BSR		

Child's Name: Marcus	**ID#:** 01-02-0222222	

Figure 8.2.   Individualized transition plan for Marcus.

for children entering kindergarten (Johnson, Gallagher, Cook, & Wong, 1995; Pianta, Cox, Taylor, & Early, 1999). Entry-level skills—skills that might facilitate a child's adjustment to his or her next learning environment—are discussed on an individual basis when conducting transition planning for a child. Because education decisions are based on a child's individual strengths and needs, as well as the experiences the child has had in the sending agency and consideration of the experiences he or she is anticipated to have in the receiving agency, no one set of skills can be called entry level. For Maria, who is making a transition from Head Start to kindergarten, entry-level skills may include independently performing self-care routines and recognizing her own name in print. Entry-level skills for Marcus, an older toddler with an identified disability, might include communicating his wants and needs through words, pictures, and/or gestures and following simple rules.

Assessing children's abilities can be accomplished through a variety of means. As programs and agencies work through the transition planning process, determination of a child's entry-level skills should be integrated into the individualized planning process. The initial step in identifying the skills that young children will need when they enter the next environment is to select some type of systematic developmental assessment system. Such a system allows for a comprehensive assessment of skills before a child exits a sending agency. The Helpful Entry-Level Skills Checklist–Revised (Byrd, Stephens, Dyk, Perry, & Rous, 1991; Rous & Hallam, 2002) and the Functional Assessment of Behavioral and Social Skills (Rous, 2001) were developed through the work of some community transition teams and highlight specific skills supported by the literature as important to children's success in the next environment, with emphasis on social, communication, and behavioral skill areas. Figure 8.3 shows a sample of the Functional Assessment of Behavioral and Social Supports.

After an assessment tool is developed or selected, procedures should be developed regarding the implementation of the assessment itself. These procedures ensure that the details of the assessment are outlined and specified for agency staff and for families served by the program. The function of a child assessment of this type is to provide educators, service providers, and families with targeted information about key skills—such as a child's social skills and ability to communicate his or her wants and needs—that will assist the child in successfully engaging in the next environment. Findings from the assessment should complement other available child assessment information and can be incorporated into regular instructional planning in the program or classroom. Guidelines should be provided to agency staff regarding the selection of targeted skills for intervention. Ideally, agency staff from both the sending and receiving agencies, as well as families, would have the opportunity to talk together regarding assessment results and plan for appropriate interventions as a team.

Teachers and caregivers can use surveys, checklists, questionnaires, and direct observations to gather information about the child's performance in the sending environment, whether that environment is a center-based classroom,

FUNCTIONAL ASSESSMENT OF BEHAVIORAL AND SOCIAL SUPPORTS

PRIORITY	SKILL	CLASSROOM RULES																	NOT PRESENT
		YES						INCONSISTENT					EMERGING						
		I	V	M	P	O*	Description of Adult or Classroom Supports	V	M	P	O*	Description of Adult Support/Nature of Inconsistency	V	M	P	O*	Description of Adult or Classroom Supports		
☐	1. Walks rather than runs indoors																		
☐	2. Waits quietly in line																		
☐	3. Sits or waits appropriately																		
☐	4. Complies with simple directions provided to a group																		
☐	5. Makes transition from one activity to another																		
☐	6. Uses appropriate behavior to get teacher attention when needed																		
☐	7. Replaces material; cleans up own activity area																		
☐	8. Stays in own space for activities																		
☐	9. Stays with group outside classroom																		

PATTERNS OF SUPPORT

KEY: I=Can perform Skill Independently   V=Need Verbal Prompt/Guidance   M=Needs Model Prompt/Guidance (peer or adult)   P=Needs Physical Prompt/Guidance
• Other Prompt -Please indicate other prompts used in Description Column (i.e. pictures, gestures)

Figure 8.3. Functional Assessment of Behavioral and Social Supports. Copyright © 2001 University of Kentucky, Interdisciplinary Human Development Institute. All rights reserved. Reprinted by permission. Except as permitted under the United States Copyright Act of 1976, no part of this publication may be reproduced or distributed in any form or by any means without the prior written permission of the publisher.

family child care home, or other type of setting. In addition, teachers and caregivers can use observations to help identify critical differences between the sending and receiving environments in which the child will be spending time.

FAMILY PREPARATION

Family involvement practices emphasize ensuring family awareness of program options and services for children and the provision of relevant information and strategies for addressing family and child needs during the transition period. For families to truly engage in the transition process, parents must have accurate information regarding relevant federal, state, community, and agency policies related to transition, as well as general information on ways to support their children's adjustment to a new environment or setting.

Developing Family Awareness of Transition and Programmatic Issues

Families should have ample opportunity to obtain the information that will help them assist their child during the transition process. Agencies can work together to develop options for increasing family awareness of transition laws and regulations and for supporting children's adjustment to new settings, such as parent trainings and informational meetings, parent-to-parent support groups, accessible written information (including family-oriented transition tools and agency web sites), and consistent information provided to families by agency staff.

Informational meetings and/or training sessions can provide a non-threatening environment for families to learn about community programs and/or parental rights. Knowledgeable speakers who can discuss the topic at hand in a family-friendly manner should conduct such sessions. Panels with representatives from multiple agencies can provide parents with comparative information on service options in the community and highlight the similarities and differences between program services. For example, the Metroville community interagency meetings, focused on kindergarten transition, were held at local preschool sites to provide parents of preschoolers with easy access to information about the upcoming kindergarten year. In addition, families who already have experienced similar transitions with their children and who are comfortable sharing their experiences often can provide helpful information to families preparing for transition. Sessions for families can be streamlined if agencies work together to combine their resources and efforts to support families in gaining access to the information they need. These streamlined sessions even can become annual events as agencies work together to ensure effective transition experiences. Some families may prefer individually planned site visits with potential new programs. Program visitation can be a powerful way for families to gain access to needed information. In the small rural community of Hobart County, individualized program visitation is a common strategy for providing parents with information about early childhood programs in the area.

In addition to transition events, agencies can develop ongoing resources to assist families. Often, programs have existing mechanisms for sharing information with families: family resource centers, programmatic web sites, family information boards, and so forth. Using these mechanisms, agencies can make available to families year-round a whole host of relevant information as families begin to plan and prepare for the transition experiences of their child. Some specific information can be particularly helpful to have on hand. For example, agencies can provide families with a list of outside agencies to provide information on family services and rights (e.g., parent training centers, other advocacy groups). In addition, brochures from potential receiving agencies can be collected, maintained, and handed out to families when transition opportunities arise. Videotaping interagency presentations or providing a series of locally developed videotapes describing program options also can be helpful to parents, while interagency newsletters that outline specific transition activities and highlight different programs also are excellent resources to keep on hand.

In addition to communitywide information on early education services, many programs have found it helpful to develop tools specifically designed for parents whose children are preparing for transition from one program to another. In particular, the development of a family transition checklist, an example of which is provided in Figure 8.4, can provide parents with information regarding documentation they will need to collect as well as activities they will need to complete to ease their child's transition into a new program. Brief summaries of the transition process that highlight key steps in implementation can remind parents of the basic steps involved in the transition to a preschool or kindergarten program (see Figure 8.5). A family handbook on transition practices is yet another method for consolidating the relevant information on early education services, legal requirements, and the procedures involved in

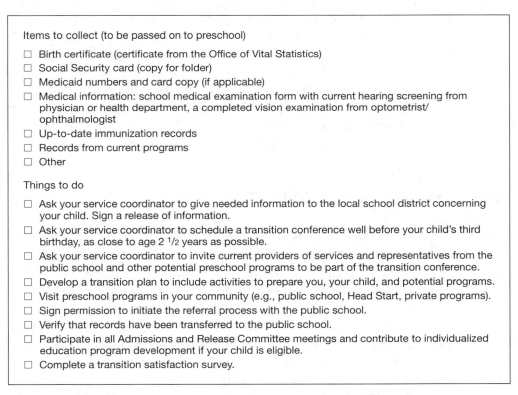

Items to collect (to be passed on to preschool)

☐ Birth certificate (certificate from the Office of Vital Statistics)
☐ Social Security card (copy for folder)
☐ Medicaid numbers and card copy (if applicable)
☐ Medical information: school medical examination form with current hearing screening from physician or health department, a completed vision examination from optometrist/ophthalmologist
☐ Up-to-date immunization records
☐ Records from current programs
☐ Other

Things to do

☐ Ask your service coordinator to give needed information to the local school district concerning your child. Sign a release of information.
☐ Ask your service coordinator to schedule a transition conference well before your child's third birthday, as close to age 2 1/2 years as possible.
☐ Ask your service coordinator to invite current providers of services and representatives from the public school and other potential preschool programs to be part of the transition conference.
☐ Develop a transition plan to include activities to prepare you, your child, and potential programs.
☐ Visit preschool programs in your community (e.g., public school, Head Start, private programs).
☐ Sign permission to initiate the referral process with the public school.
☐ Verify that records have been transferred to the public school.
☐ Participate in all Admissions and Release Committee meetings and contribute to individualized education program development if your child is eligible.
☐ Complete a transition satisfaction survey.

Figure 8.4. Family transition checklist. (From Kentucky Early Childhood Transition Project. [1995]. *Step by step: A family guide for transition into preschool.* Lexington: University of Kentucky, Human Development Institute; adapted by permission.)

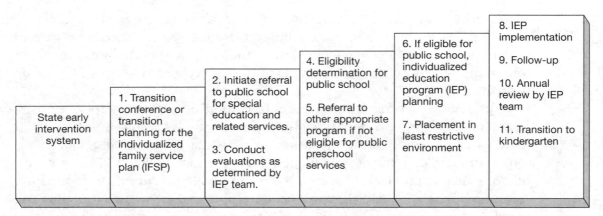

Figure 8.5.   Basic steps in the transition from early intervention to preschool.

transition. This type of resource is particularly helpful for parents of children with disabilities who need to understand the way in which federal, state, and local policies intersect and are implemented in their community and specifically for their child (see Figure 8.6). Such family-oriented tools encourage family participation in the transition process as well as reinforce the notion that parents are critical players in transition planning for their children.

Agency staff often provide the most information to families, so agency and program staff must have accurate and up-to-date information on relevant transition topics. As described in Chapter 7, staff professional development should include key transition topics for families, including federal regulations and guidelines for transition, basic information concerning other program options, and strategies to support children's adjustment to new settings.

Involving Families in Their Child's Transition

Successful transitions involve families as meaningful partners in the planning process. Agencies can outline appropriate methods and strategies for providing detailed descriptions of family roles and responsibilities in the transition process. Specifically, families should be involved in the transition meeting, acquiring information about possible postprogram options, and the referral and evaluation processes. Meaningful family participation in the transition process can enhance a family's ability to support their child in the next environment. A parent with accurate programmatic information can feel more comfortable as his or her child enters a new program. Thus, agency procedures that outline myriad options for family participation increase the likelihood that family participation will occur.

TABLE OF CONTENTS

Figure 8.6. Contents of transition handbook for parents. (From Kentucky Early Childhood Transition Project. [1995]. *Step by step: A family guide for transition into preschool.* Lexington: University of Kentucky, Human Development Institute; adapted by permission.)

• • •

Maria's mother began to discuss the transition to kindergarten with the Head Start family service worker in January of Maria's preschool year. As the staff provided information to help her better understand the importance of being involved in Maria's educational process and tips for preparing Maria for transition into kindergarten, Juanita began to better understand her role and responsibilities in the transition process. She gave permission to the Head Start staff to share information about Maria's educational needs to the public school, and the Head Start family service worker referred Juanita to the school family resource center so that she could continue to receive information and support for her other family needs.

• • •

Information and Strategies for Addressing Family Needs

Just as children need additional support and planning during times of transition, so do parents. Considering the needs of families and children during transition planning is important. To address family needs, agencies can outline policies for ensuring that families have access to information and additional services that may be needed during the transition process as well as in the next environment. Agency policies should address both child-specific information and information and referrals to needed family services.

Provide Information to Families Families should be considered a critical part of the assessment process. Agencies should provide clear procedures and a process for including families in the assessment process, securing family input in prioritizing and targeting skills related to transition, and providing families with information and strategies for supporting and reinforcing skill development at home.

Develop Procedures for Linking Families to Needed Supplemental Services Some families may need additional resources as they prepare for their child's transition. Information about and referral for transportation, housing, or social services may be needed. Both sending and receiving agencies should consider the potential for these additional needs in their transition planning. Agencies can develop methods for information sharing regarding access to supplemental services in the community. Community interagency groups often develop resource guides that include contact information, types of services provided, and eligibility requirements. This type of information can be particularly useful at this point in the transition planning process. In Hobart County, the development of a community resource guide was the first outcome of the community interagency group. It provides a very useful resource for families and agencies in understanding agency resources in the community.

The development of procedures in agencies should provide a mechanism to ensure that agency staff inquire about supplemental family needs, provide support to families having those needs met, and follow-up to ensure that the needed services were received.

SUMMARY

Implementing specific strategies to support child and family preparation is essential to an effective transition process. Planning for transition needs to address the unique needs of children and families as well as the more general structural needs that will arise during the transition planning process. Communities that are prepared for both can more easily navigate community resources to support young children and families as they transition across programs.

Chapter 9

Written Guidance

Mrs. Martino teaches in Metroville in the Head Start program. This spring, Alex's mother, Monica, approached Mrs. Martino about how the Head Start staff were helping Alex get ready for kindergarten in the fall and how she could help Alex. Mrs. Martino was a bit stumped. She and her assistant teacher had talked about the transition to kindergarten a little, and she knew it was important, but she really had not thought about how the family could help. Mrs. Martino looked through all of her orientation materials and the program policies and procedures but could not find any information on what she was expected to do for transition planning.

• • •

Teachers may look to program policies and procedures for guidance on how to address a specific request or issue that arises in the classroom. In this case, the Head Start program's lack of policies or materials leaves Mrs. Martino little guidance on how to address Monica's request for information on how she can best support Alex's transition to kindergarten. To meet the request, Mrs. Martino would need to spend countless hours either researching the program resources and approach or developing her own resources or materials. Should Mrs. Martino choose to develop her own materials and processes, her approach may not be consistent with others that have been developed in different classrooms in the building, program, or other programs in the community.

Research has indicated that for a transition process to be effective, it should be comprehensive and support continuity between programs (Love, Logue, Trudeau, & Thayer, 1992; National Center for Early Development and Learning, 1999; Rous, Hemmeter, & Schuster, 1994). In other words, good transition planning depends on collaboration among agency staff within and across programs, families, and communities (Jang & Mangione, 1994; Rice & O'Brien, 1990; Rous et al., 1994; Rous, Hemmeter, & Schuster, 1999). This includes *intra-agency collaboration*, collaboration within a specific program or agency, and *interagency collaboration*, collaboration across various agencies and programs. Both types of collaboration are critical in addressing the needs of children and families so that children can meet success in their next environments (Rosenkoetter, Hains, & Fowler, 1994).

Because the transition process for young children involves multiple early childhood agencies and programs, such as child care, Head Start, and public preschools, the success of the transition process partially depends on the ability of the program administration to provide clear and concise written guidance that supports staff, families, and children during the transition period. This chapter presents a team process that can be used to determine the most appropriate type of written guidance for supporting interagency and intra-agency practices and activities developed and implemented by the transition team.

THE IMPORTANCE OF WRITTEN GUIDANCE

Written guidance plays an important role in helping teachers, staff, families, and others understand their roles and responsibilities related to transition practices and activities. General written guidance in the form of policies and procedures can have a positive impact on program and practice implementation when the content of the policy is clear and specificity within the policies is appropriate (Sabatier & Mazmanian, 1979; Williams, 1971). Another important aspect of written guidance is the role of policy in helping to ensure that evidence-based and recommended practices are implemented within the program (Harbin & Salisbury, 2000). Written guidance is especially critical when new staff are hired so that they have specific information on the type of transition activities and supports to be provided to the children and families they serve. In most programs, a number of transition practices and activities already are in place and being implemented by staff. Many times, however, these practices and activities fall into one of three categories.

Agency personnel use a variety of strategies and activities without having written information available to support and institutionalize those practices.

● ● ●

Staff in the Metroville early intervention program have regularly invited the preschool coordinator from Metroville Public Schools to attend transition conferences, and she has always tried to attend. This year, the district hired new central office staff to oversee the federal programs, including the preschool program. As a result, the preschool coordinator was given additional assignments and was told she could no longer attend the transition meetings on a regular basis.

● ● ●

In this case, the practice of including the preschool coordinator in transition conferences was not included in a written agreement between the early intervention program and the public school, which resulted in a discontinuation of a successful practice. Without written guidance—in this case, an interagency agreement—the preschool coordinator may have little recourse with her new supervisor in continuing the practice.

Agency personnel, teachers, and staff members use different transition strategies and activities.

● ● ●

Jennifer, Marcus's service coordinator, arranged for his parents, Sarah and Joe, to visit both the Hobart County public preschool program and the Head Start program as part of their transition-planning activities. One week after Jennifer worked with Sarah and Joe to schedule the visits, Claudia, Marcus's speech therapist, mentioned to Sarah and Joe that they should get in touch with some of the other parents whose children are participating in the public school preschool program to discuss what the program is like before they make a visit. Sarah and Joe are now a bit confused because they have already arranged their schedules to visit the programs the next day.

● ● ●

In this case, two of Marcus's providers have provided conflicting information to the family on strategies for preparing for the transition process. Although both strategies have merit, the lack of congruency or coordination between the providers has left the parents confused and anxious about whether they are taking the right approach. Providing clear, written guidance to agency staff about the specific transition activities and strategies that should be provided, along with information on who should provide the information, can help alleviate confusion on the part of staff and parents.

Agencies and programs have developed their own policies and guidance documents to support specific practices and activities without input from other agencies affected by or participating in the transition activities.

• • •

The Hobart County early intervention program has indicated in their procedures that staff should send specific information to the public school system about children who will be making the transition to preschool. However, this information was included in the agency's procedures without discussing it with the public preschool administration. Therefore, when Mrs. Howard, a preschool teacher, received the information about Marcus, she filed it away and it was never used.

• • •

In this case, it is clear that the early intervention program administration developed their own policies and guidance documents without input from other agencies affected by or participating in the transition activities. Although having written guidance within an agency is important, if the activities affect or require the participation of individuals in another agency, the issues should be discussed on an interagency basis so that written guidance is congruent. For example, written guidance to support transition process policies should include specifics about the most appropriate information to include in packets sent to the receiving agency and the mechanism to use for the transmittal of the information so that it is timely, meaningful, and useful to the new program and staff. As a result, receiving agencies or programs are aware of and able to more actively participate in the specific transition practice or activity.

COLLABORATIVE DEVELOPMENT OF WRITTEN GUIDANCE MATERIALS

Because the success of the transition experience depends on communication and collaboration among agency staff, the collaborative establishment and implementation of transition policies and procedures that cross programs (Conn-Powers, Ross-Allen, & Holburn, 1990; Hanline, 1993; Rous et al., 1999) and that support shared leadership, decision making, and program evaluation (Jang & Mangione, 1994) can help ease the transition process for families that move between and among these various agencies. Specifically, collaborative activities and roles related to the development of written procedures for specific tasks, timelines, and responsibilities that help staff plan for transition are recommended (Rice & O'Brien, 1990).

Without collaborative development of transition policies and procedures, a lack of congruency often exists across agencies in terms of practices, policies, and procedures. This can result in administrators, staff, and even families working at cross-purposes and in duplication of services and supports. Worse yet, a gap in or loss of services for the child and family following the transition could result. However, policies and procedures that are discussed and developed on a collaborative basis can reduce traditional barriers to planning and collaboration, such as disagreement about policy implementation and responsibilities, duplication of services, and lack of knowledge of other parts of the system (Rice & O'Brien, 1990).

In some situations, developing one document that is adopted and used by all agencies participating in the transition planning process may be appropriate. For example, the interagency transition team may determine that direct services staff need assistance with developing transition outcomes for young children with disabilities. This type of written document would be developed by the interagency transition team and approved for use through the appropriate administrative channels within individual agencies. In this case, each program may need to address the use of the document in their agency policies and procedures.

TYPES OF WRITTEN GUIDANCE

As discussed previously, the use of written guidance plays an important role in ensuring successful transitions for staff, families, and children. Written guidance can be provided in a number of ways to help formalize transition practices and support congruency across agencies and programs. Three categories of written documentation—each of which are described in detail next—have been used most frequently to support transition activities: 1) policies, regulations, and procedures; 2) interagency agreements; and 3) technical guidance documents such as transition plans, training manuals, technical assistance documents, and family handbooks.

Policies, Regulations, and Procedures

Policies, regulations, and procedures are the most common forms of written guidance used in programs, and they can be very effective in supporting the transition process. *Policies* provide a framework for translating the philosophy and approach that an agency is taking related to services. Policies help ensure that appropriate services and practices are implemented in a program and that a program's desired outcomes are met. According to Gallagher (1994), policies should be written so that they answer the following questions:

- Who receives the resources or service?

- Who delivers the resources or service?

- Which specific resources or services are to be delivered?

- What are the conditions under which the resources or services are delivered?

In the area of transition, agencies already may have specific transition policies in place, many of which are linked to federal and/or state regulations that guide the transition process. For example, under the Individuals with Disabilities Education Improvement Act (IDEA) of 2004 (PL 108-446), early intervention providers must convene a transition conference to help the family and child plan for the child's transition at age 3. Therefore, early intervention programs should include a policy that addresses the requirement for a transition conference.

Regulations are rules, directives, statutes, and/or standards that govern early childhood programs. Regulations related to transition are provided for children with disabilities through IDEA of 2004 (see Figure 3.8 in Chapter 3). Head Start programs also have Performance Standards (45 CFR Part 1308) that provide guidance to programs in the area of transition, and the No Child Left Behind Act's Good Start Grow Smart also emphasizes collaboration and transition (see Figures 3.9 and 3.10 in Chapter 3). State-specific programs, such as child care or state-funded preschool programs, also may have regulations that have been developed at the state level to provide guidance and support in transition planning.

Procedures are based on agency policies and provide specific guidance on how to implement the policy. Procedures should be developed and evaluated regularly so that they can change over time as new techniques are learned and new activities are designed or as situations change. In the area of transition, procedures should focus on identifying specific tasks, timelines, and responsibilities related to the practices and activities adopted by the agency or program.

● ● ●

The Metroville early intervention program conducted a series of evaluations and assessments to determine Maria's developmental status prior to leaving the early intervention system at age 3. Maria and her family were referred to her local public school for services, but for some reason, her evaluation information was not shared.

● ● ●

Tyler underwent numerous evaluations in the Hobart County Head Start program. At age 5, he was referred to his local public school for services, where identical evaluations were completed by the Hobart County school system.

● ● ●

As demonstrated in this example, the staff in these programs followed specific regulations and requirements for conducting appropriate evaluations to determine eligibility for their respective programs. Because the programs lacked specific procedures related to the sharing of evaluation information among agencies as part of the transition process, however, duplicative and uncoordinated evaluations resulted for both Maria and Tyler. This duplication of efforts can be stressful for the family and the child and confusing for service providers. In Tyler's case, the reliability and validity of evaluation information also was jeopardized.

Interagency Policies and Procedures The previous vignettes demonstrate the need for coordination in the development of transition-related policies and procedures. Interagency policies and procedures are agency-specific procedures that have been discussed, refined, and/or recommended by the interagency transition team after agreement is reached on the key issues and processes. Interagency policies and procedures are important when specific services that are implemented in one agency directly affect another agency. In the case of the agencies in the previous vignettes, the transition team may recommend a set of policies and procedures for Head Start, early intervention, and the public school that outline the specific roles and responsibilities of each agency in sharing evaluation information.

In many agencies, especially larger organizations, specific guidelines exist for the way in which policies and procedures are developed and approved. Therefore, the role of the interagency transition team is to determine whether an agency needs additional policies to support new transition activities or respond to new regulations and/or whether an agency needs to develop or revise procedures to support new or existing policies. The members of the interagency team then can make specific recommendations to their agencies or programs about policies and procedures that can help support continuity of services across agencies. Depending on the issue being addressed, the transition team may choose to involve additional people in a working group whose purpose will be to make recommendations about specific policies and procedures. For example, in the previous case, the school psychologists and others who conduct the evaluations, the teachers who receive the evaluation information, and the family members may be asked to participate in the process of refining and developing the suggested procedures.

Tips for Writing Transition Policies and Procedures Policies and procedures can take a variety of formats, depending on program or agency guidelines. However, some characteristics of good policies and procedures hold true across program types. Policies should

- Be written using clear, concise, and simple language

- Provide information on the specific rule and not provide detailed information on how to implement the rule

- Be written in a way that is not unnecessarily restrictive and that provides some options for implementation

Procedures should

- Be tied to a specific policy

- Be written in a way that is easily understandable and that can be followed by a variety of people in the organization

- Be written with input from a variety of stakeholders so that the program staff feel a sense of ownership

Interagency Agreements

The second type of written guidance that can be helpful in the area of transition is interagency agreements. Written interagency agreements can be used to provide guidelines and information regarding how agencies can work together to support the transition process. An interagency agreement usually refers to a more formalized written document that is signed by upper administrative personnel in an agency or program. Interagency agreements are appropriate in several situations related to the transition process.

First, interagency agreements can be used to create a new activity or event that has been identified and developed by the team. For example, the transition team may determine that joint screening of young children is an important interagency activity. An agreement would be useful in defining who is responsible for what during the process. Second, interagency agreements can be used to ensure that specific activities and events planned and implemented by the team continue. An example would be specific roles and responsibilities of each agency and program in helping to find and identify young children who need early intervention or specialized services and supports, otherwise known as Child Find.

Some early childhood programs—early intervention, Head Start, and public preschool programs for young children with disabilities—have very specific requirements about the use of interagency agreements and items that should be included. Hadden, Fowler, Fink, and Wischnowski (1995) found that interagency agreements were specifically useful in supporting the transmittal of information among agencies and in addressing how assessment and eligibility information can be coordinated and shared across programs.

Three major components should be included in interagency agreements. First, interagency agreements should include specific language around actions, roles, and responsibilities of agencies and personnel in those agencies. Second, they should include information related to the financial and resource commitment of each agency and/or program as it relates to the activity or activities addressed in the agreement. Third, the agreement should include information on the time frame for which the agreement will be in effect. Table 9.1 presents a list of exemplary provisions required for the transition process.

Table 9.1. Example of provisions for the transition process addressed in an interagency agreement

	Early intervention	Local school district	Head Start	Other sending/receiving agencies	Families
Child Find	Provides child list without identifying information; coordinates Child Find activities	Uses child information for program planning; coordinates Child Find activities	Makes referrals to early intervention/districts; collaborates with Child Find activities	Makes referrals to early intervention/districts	Shares information about current program with other parents
Transition conference	Schedules/conducts/develops/implements transition plan for family support/child preparation/receiving agency preparation	Attends/actively participates in/implements transition plan for family support/child preparation/staff preparation	Participates as appropriate	Participates as appropriate	Gives permission and participates fully in implementation of transition plan
Referral process	Initiates intake/referral notification	Receives/completes/acts	Participates as appropriate	Participates as appropriate	Gives permission and participates fully
Initial IEP committee	Participates in individualized education program (IEP) process	Schedules/conducts IEP meeting	Participates as appropriate	Participates as appropriate	Attends meetings and participates fully in IEP process
Implementation and follow-up	Implements/participates in follow-up as appropriate	Implements/participates in follow-up	Participates as appropriate	Participates as appropriate	Supports implementation of individualized family service plan transition plan and the IEP (as eligible); participates by completing follow-up parent survey

Using the following FACTS will help ensure that all guidance documents, regardless of type, are written in a way that will support recommended transition activities.

- **F**actual information is a must. Check and recheck for accuracy of information, and ensure that policies accurately reflect appropriate regulations and that procedures appropriately represent policies.

- **A**cronyms should be spelled out the first time they are used.

- **C**oncise information is best; use a minimum number of words.

- **T**imely information is important, but do not include information that will be quickly outdated, such as people's names (use positions instead).

- **S**imple is better. Keep technical words to a minimum so that families and new staff members can understand information.

Technical Guidance Documents

Technical guidance documents are those that are developed to support the transition process for families and staff and provide more detailed information to support implementation. For example, transition plans, training manuals, technical assistance documents, and family handbooks can be considered technical documents. The overall purpose of a technical guidance document is to provide additional materials to support the implementation of specific policies, regulations, and procedures or to support carrying out specific activities that have been identified in a written interagency agreement.

● ● ●

Over the past year, the Metroville interagency transition team has been working on their interagency agreement related to addressing the IDEA regulations for the transition process between early intervention and preschool services. As a result, they have determined that one of the critical needs is to better support families in the transition from early intervention to preschool. To address this need, they have decided to develop a family handbook for transition.

● ● ●

In this example, a family handbook would serve as a technical guidance document. The purpose of the handbook would be to describe to families the transition activities that they can engage in to support their child's transition from early intervention to public preschool. This handbook would address specific questions in family-friendly language, such as, "What is preschool?" "What does the Metroville preschool program look like?" and "How can my family support my child's transition?"

● ● ●

The Hobart County transition team has been working over the last year to find ways to better support families as their children prepare to make the transition from preschool to kindergarten. As part of this process, they developed a community transition plan that included specific activities and strategies for supporting the kindergarten transition.

● ● ●

Another common type of technical guidance document is community or program transition plans. Transition plans are written documents that are based on either community or local program transition needs and typically list strategies and activities that are being implemented to meet identified transition needs, timelines for the activities, individuals responsible, and how the activity or strategy will be evaluated and revised. Transition plans may be developed at a community level by interagency partners to support interagency activities and at a program level to further define the specific role and implementation process for activities that are outlined in the broader community plan. The plans then can serve as guiding documents for the team or staff as they implement activities. In addition, they can be useful in helping to keep other stakeholders apprised of the activities of the transition team.

● ● ●

Last week, one of the members of the local school board read an article in the paper about the importance of school readiness and became interested in what the school system was doing to better support the transition to kindergarten. As a result, the superintendent asked the team to provide some specific information about their activities as part of the school board report. Because the Hobart County team developed a community plan that included specific activities to support the transition to kindergarten, the team was able to share these plans with the school board to help document activities that were in place to support school readiness.

● ● ●

A number of activities and strategies might be included in a community transition plan. These include the following:

- A community transition calendar of events

- Information about interagency training for all programs involved with age-3 transitions

- Steps for revising a local interagency agreement

- Information about community open house for transition orientation for preschool and/or kindergarten families

- Information about a family visitation or activity with kindergarten programs

- A rotation for staff visitation among programs

Community or program transition plans should not be confused with individual transition plans for children or families. Specific activities may be included in a community or program plan to prepare children and families in programs and communities, but this is not the place to detail specific children and their individual goals or activities. More information related to individual child and family transition plans is provided in Chapter 7.

NEGOTIATING AND DEVELOPING TRANSITION ACTIVITIES AND PROCESSES

Numerous strategies and activities can be implemented to support the transition process for children and families. The written guidance for these strategies and practices provides the foundation for their implementation by staff, families, and children. Keys for the development of congruent strategies and practices include the following:

1. Strategies and practices are discussed and negotiated by all members of the transition team.

2. Specific decisions are made about how each agency will implement the practice in ways that are congruent and coordinated.

3. Decisions by the team are formalized and/or supported with written guidance.

As the transition team develops transition activities, five steps, illustrated in Figure 9.1, support this process:

1. **Identify current status across agencies.** For each area (e.g., evaluations of young children at transition points), the team should identify what

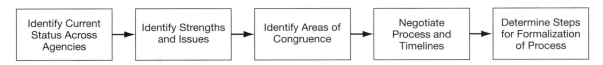

Figure 9.1. Steps for negotiating and developing transition activities and processes.

each agency currently has in place. If written materials are available within the agency that describe the process (e.g., policies, procedures, guidelines, forms), these materials should be made available to the other members of the team during the discussion. In addition, team members should identify any state or federal regulations for which they are responsible in the area. This allows the team members an opportunity to identify those activities and processes that are negotiable and those that are not. Using the team recording process discussed in Chapter 7 will help the team keep track of what each agency currently has in place.

2. **Identify current strengths and issues.** Individual team members should discuss the effectiveness of their current process, including their perspective of their process's strengths and concerns. If the interagency team has identified a list of barriers, as discussed in Chapter 6, they can identify those specific barriers that are related to the area under discussion.

3. **Identify areas of congruence.** As a team, identify consistent or similar processes or activities that cross agencies. By doing this, the team can reduce the number of brand new strategies and activities to be implemented and can instead refine activities that may already be in place in some form or fashion within several agencies. This allows the team to build new processes by pulling out the most successful components of the activities that are currently in place.

4. **Negotiate process and timelines.** As a team, identify and negotiate specific processes that will 1) address barriers identified by the team, 2) build on current activities and processes that are in place across agencies, 3) take into consideration the strengths of similar processes that are already in place and address any issues that have been identified, and 4) allow for a more congruent process that can be used across agencies and programs.

5. **Identify steps for formalization of the process.** As a team, identify the specific steps that need to take place to formalize recommendations with each agency. Discuss timelines and activities related to how and when the process for formalization will be completed.

This same process can be used across multiple activities as they are identified for implementation by the transition team. To help institutionalize

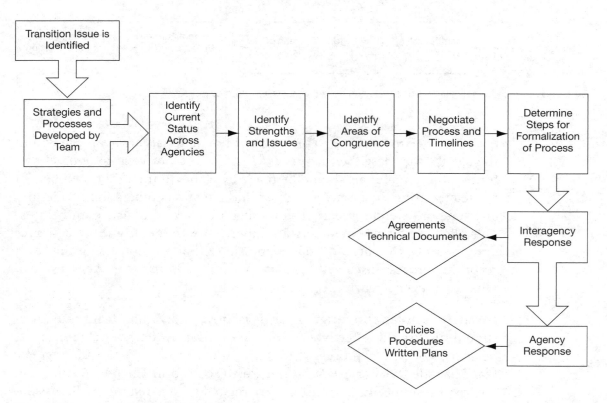

Figure 9.2.   Process for formalization of transition activities.

transition activities and processes that have been negotiated and developed between agencies and programs, the transition team should make decisions on
how the final activities and processes will be formalized both within the individual agencies and across agencies (see Figure 9.2).

• • •

Over the past year, the Hobart County transition team has been working on identifying specific strategies that address the issue of duplication of evaluations for children
as they transition from early intervention to preschool and from preschool to kindergarten. Prior to beginning their work, early intervention providers often complained
that they worked hard to conduct exit evaluations that were never used by the preschool staff. In turn, preschool teachers complained that they worked hard to complete evaluations that the school psychologists often repeated during the first few
months of the kindergarten year.

• • •

To help address these issues and concerns, the transition team identified
two strategies that might work. First, they identified specific evaluation pro-

cesses and timelines that were currently required in the early intervention, preschool, and kindergarten programs. Based on these requirements, they identified the specific evaluation tools that were used by each agency. Using this information, they came up with a set of procedures for how evaluation information could be shared across agencies, including how and by whom the evaluation would need to be conducted to be acceptable to the receiving agency.

Second, they developed a set of procedures that could be implemented within each agency to support the sharing of information about previous evaluation data that might be helpful to the receiving staff. This included specific steps on how the information would be shared, by whom, in what format, and when.

Specific recommendations for integrating these new procedures were presented to the administrative staff in each agency, and timelines were negotiated. Training on the new procedures was then provided to appropriate staff members across the agencies. As a result of the new procedures, teachers indicated that in most cases they were able to use the information provided by sending agency staff without feeling the need to re-administer all of their own evaluations and assessments.

SUMMARY

Agency policies, procedures, and written guidance materials often are used in agencies to support recommended practices and activities. This chapter provided strategies and ideas for how to develop policies, procedures, and guidance materials that better support the transition process through collaborative development and integration across the multiple agencies that provide services to young children and families. This written guidance can in turn help teachers, staff, families, and others better understand their roles and responsibilities related to transition practices and activities.

Chapter 10

Developing the Plan

Maria had just accepted a position at the Metroville Public Schools. She was excited about her new job as the Preschool Coordinator for the district. At the end of her first month, she received two important telephone calls. The first was from the assistant superintendent. He told her that at the last school board meeting, a recent article in the local paper about school readiness prompted the board members to ask for information about how the district was addressing issues related to school readiness and the transition of young children into kindergarten. He asked her to gather information to present at the next school board meeting. The second telephone call was from Claire, the Metroville Head Start Director, inviting her to attend their next local transition team meeting. What timing! They set up an appointment so that Claire could provide some background information on the community transition team and introduce Maria to the current plan of action.

• • •

Action or work plans have long been used to help teams and groups formalize specific actions they wish to take to meet a set of goals or objectives and to lend credibility to the work of the team. The use of a work plan by the transition team demonstrates to others in the community that the team is well-organized and dedicated to accomplishing activities they have identified as important. A community transition work plan is also useful in

1. Helping the team ensure that they have not forgotten any details that might derail the activities they have chosen to implement

2. Increasing the efficiency of the team by reducing duplication of effort and use of resources and energy

3. Increasing the chances that team members will complete identified tasks, thereby helping to keep the team accountable for actions and outcomes

Numerous formats and processes have been used to complete work plans. However, work plans generally address some common questions:

1. *What* activity, action, or change will occur?

2. *Who* will carry it out?

3. *When* will it take place, and for how long?

4. *What* resources (e.g., money, staff) are needed to carry out the change?

5. *How* will the plan be evaluated to determine completion?

Work plans are not static but rather dynamic and should change and grow as the team identifies new barriers and practices to implement. Work plans are most effective when developed as annual plans. Teams need to choose a time of year to review the current plan, make appropriate changes and document progress, and then select new practices to implement to address ongoing barriers or, in some cases, identify new barriers that need to be addressed.

SELECTING TRANSITION BARRIERS TO ADDRESS

Chapter 6 outlined a process that the interagency team can use to identify the major barriers to successful transitions in the community and to assess the current status of transition activities. Although all of the barriers that the team identifies are important, the team should start the planning process by prioritizing those barriers that are currently the most critical or those that have the greatest negative impact on the transition process for children and families.

When selecting critical barriers to address, three approaches can be used, either in isolation or in combination.

1. Select barriers that can be addressed most easily. This is especially helpful for new teams because it gives them some success on which they can build as they begin to address more complex or difficult tasks. An example of an easy barrier would be a lack of staff knowledge about the programs and services available in the community.

2. Identify areas in which agencies and programs may not be meeting mandated requirements or regulations. This may be helpful if the agencies involved on the transition team are under directives to address these issues due to a recent or upcoming monitoring visit. For example, the community may not have in place an interagency agreement, which is required for the early intervention and Head Start programs.

3. Identify those barriers that are most salient to staff and families in the agencies represented on the transition team. This approach would require some form of survey or community forum to determine which barriers seem most critical to staff and families. This gives the transition team a more detailed or narrow list of barriers from which they can begin to link potential strategies and activities.

No matter which approach is used, the team's list of barriers will probably be too long to address all of the barriers at one time, and the team may need to prioritize the list of barriers to determine where to start. The team should review the process put into place for prioritizing goals and activities (see Chapter 5) and use this process to rank the barriers starting with those that are most critical. For example, the Metroville interagency transition team identified a list of barriers that were seen as important to families, staff, and administrators across programs (see Figure 10.1). Based on this list, they used dotting (see Chapter 5, pages 72–73) as a way to narrow the list to three barriers that were most critical to address first. A blank, photocopiable form is provided on page 183 in the appendix.

LINKING TRANSITION ACTIVITIES TO BARRIERS

With information in hand about the critical barriers that need to be addressed, the team can link specific barriers to activities or practices that can be implemented to address these barriers. Figure 10.2—completed for the

Prioritizing Barriers to Transition

Barriers to transition	Priority barriers based on dotting approach
Information about children making transitions into new programs is not shared.	Information about children making transitions into new programs is not shared.
Teachers have different expectations and philosophies about what and how children learn.	
Agencies have different and often conflicting enrollment and referral procedures and timelines.	Agencies have different and often conflicting enrollment and referral procedures and timelines.
Staff are unclear about program options for children and families after the transition.	Staff are unclear about program options for children and families after the transition.
Transportation for children with significant disabilities is not available.	
Receiving programs do not accept evaluation information for children entering programs from the sending agency.	
Families are not aware of differences between sending and receiving programs.	
Children with significant disabilities do not bring augmentative and alternative communication or other equipment with them to the new programs.	
Teachers do not have the opportunity to see other programs into which their children go after transition.	

Figure 10.1. Prioritized list of barriers to transition. Sample: Metroville, USA.

Metroville interagency team and provided as a blank form on pages 184–185 in the appendix—provides a format for linking barriers to the specific transition practices discussed in Chapters 7 and 8. The team should use the list of barriers that were identified by the team in Chapter 6 and match those barriers to activities or practices that could help them. It is probable that more than one practice can address a barrier and that some barriers can be addressed through multiple practices. The team should use the interagency structure (see Chapter 4) put into place to help them discuss the available options and to make deci-

Linking Barriers to Transition Practices

Instructions: Using the list of barriers identified by the team, match barriers to those activities or practices that could help address the barriers. More than one barrier may be addressed through an activity, and some barriers can be addressed through multiple activities.

Transition practice or activity	Specific barriers addressed	
1. Staff have key information about agencies and services available in the community.	Staff are unclear about program options for children and families.	
2. A single contact person for transition is identified from each agency.	Information about children making transitions into new programs is not shared.	
3. Broad-based transition activities and timelines are identified (e.g., open house, Child Find).	Agencies have different and often conflicting enrollment and referral procedures and timelines.	Agencies have different and often conflicting enrollment and referral procedures and timelines.
4. Processes are in place for child- and family-based transition meetings.		
5. Processes are in place for enrollment and referral.	Agencies have different referral procedures and timelines.	
6. Processes are in place for screenings and evaluations.		
7. Processes are in place for follow-up on children in transition.	Information about children making transitions into new programs is not shared.	
8. Processes are in place to ensure that staff and family members are actively involved in transition system design.		
9. Staff roles and responsibilities for transition activities are outlined.		
10. There is continuity in curriculum and child expectations.		

Figure 10.2. Linking barriers to transition practices. Sample: Metroville, USA.

(continued)

147

Figure 10.2. *(continued)*

Item		
11. Methods are in place to support staff-to-staff communication.	*Information about children making transitions into new programs is not shared.*	
12. Information about children making a transition is shared.	*Information about children making transitions into new programs is not shared.*	
13. Individual transition plans are developed for each child and family.		
14. Children have opportunities to develop the entry-level skills they need to be successful in the receiving environment.		
15. Families are aware of the importance of transition planning and have the information they need to actively participate in transition planning with their child.	*Staff are unclear about program options for children and families.*	
16. Families participate as partners with staff in transition-planning activities.		
17. Families' needs related to transition are assessed and addressed.		
18. Families actively participate in gathering information about their child's growth and development.		
19. Families have information about additional resources and services to help them meet their specific child and family needs.	*Staff are unclear about program options for children and families*	

148

sions (see Chapter 5) about which activities hold the most promise in meeting the barriers identified in their community. No two community plans are or should be alike. The type of practices selected will depend on the community demographics and the service system in place in the community. In addition, the activities chosen should reflect those in which the team may already have had some success by at least one agency in putting the specific practice into place. The team can refer to Figure 6.2 and Figure 6.3 to determine which practices may already have been implemented and might be refined to meet the needs of other agencies represented on the team.

DEVELOPING THE WORK PLAN

Once a list of potential practices has been identified, the team must select the specific practices they will implement as a community team. Recommended steps for implementing a practice can be found in Chapters 6 and 7 and can be adapted and refined in the work plan. The Community Transition Team Work Plan—a completed example of which is provided in Figure 10.3 and a blank copy of which is provided on pages 186–188 in the appendix—has three parts. The cover page provides space to put the name of the team, date of the plan, team member names/agencies, transition definition, tran-sition points addressed, and community vision, all of which are addressed in Chapter 3.

The second part of the plan provides information on six critical components of the plan that should be determined for each barrier that will be addressed.

1. *Needs statement:* The needs statement is based on the barrier to be addressed by the team. It answers the question, "What is the barrier or problem?" In the example in Figure 10.3, the Metroville interagency transition team identified one critical barrier as "Staff are unclear about program options for children and families." Therefore, the needs statement could be "Staff need consistent information about program options for children and families making a transition."

2. *Expected outcomes:* The expected outcomes component should answer the question, "What will be in place after the team completes the work?" The team should think in terms of concrete, specific products, policies, and/or procedures. The expected outcomes should come directly from the practice(s) the team has selected to implement to address the barrier. For example, in Metroville the team chose to start with the practice, "Staff have key information about agencies and services available in the community" to address the barrier presented previously. As a result of reviewing the information presented in Chapter 7, the team identified the expected

Community Transition Team Work Plan

Community: Metroville   **Date:** August 2005

Team members:

1. Mary—Early intervention program
2. Claire—Metroville Schools
3. John—Head Start director
4. Sue—Young Kid Child Care
5. Maria—Family representative
6. Mike—Health department
7.
8.

Transition definition:
Transition is the process of moving among agencies, programs, and services.

Transition points addressed:
We will concentrate on providing a smooth transition for children between birth and 5 years of age.

Community vision statement:
The Metroville transition team will focus on developing a partnership between families and service providers that enhances the transition process for all young children, including those children with developmental disabilities. Through a cooperative effort, agencies will strive to serve as a transition resource and expand options to continually meet the changing needs of children and families.

Needs statement Statement of barriers to overcome	Staff need consistent information about program options for children and families making a transition.
Expected outcomes Products, events, and so forth that will be in place in response to the barrier	A resource directory is available and updated annually to provide information about services available in Metroville.
Expected impact Change brought about as results of outcomes	Staff have key information about agencies and services available in the community that they can share with families during the transition process. Families have information about their options for services when the child makes transitions and information about other services and supports in the community that can help them meet their needs.
Stakeholders/ method of involvement (e.g., surveys, focus group interviews, advisory committees)	Teachers and providers: Representatives serve on workgroup, review and input into directory, and participate in training. Transition team: Representatives serve on transition team and workgroup, and review and input into directory. Administrators: Representatives review and input and approve policy and procedures. Families: Members review and input into directory.
Resources and supports Resources that can be tapped for assistance	Resource notebook available through the Family Resource Center Technology staff at Metroville Schools Sample resource booklets available through National Transition Center and SERVE Terrific Transition web sites
Evaluation of outcomes Methods used to determine that expected outcomes have been achieved	Follow-up survey with teachers to determine use and helpfulness of resource booklet Policies and procedures in place for use of the resource book across agencies Follow-up survey with families on access to services

Action Plan

Outcome/objective: Develop resource directory for Metroville

Steps/activities needed for implementation	Timelines	Person responsible
1. Establish a small workgroup and present charge and timelines.	9/06	Transition team
2. Develop a list of agencies providing services to children and families.	10/06	Workgroup
3. Conduct a survey with each relevant agency to identify • Services provided • How eligibility is determined (federal and state mandates followed) • Funding for the agency and fees charged to consumers • The population served by the agency • The agency philosophy	10/06–12/06	Workgroup
4. Determine the best mechanism for formalizing the information and sharing with staff.	1/07	Workgroup
5. Determine which staff members need access to the information.	1/07	Workgroup
6. Determine a process for updating information about agencies on a regular basis.	2/07	Workgroup
7. Develop and recommend agency policies, procedures, or guidelines that address how the transition resource materials will be used in each agency to facilitate the transition.	5/07	Transition team
8. Provide information and/or training to staff about the resource directory or other materials and expectations for their use.	5/07–6/07	Transition team

Figure 10.3. Community transition team work plan. Sample: Metroville, USA.

outcome as resource directory that would be shared across programs and staff.

3. *Expected impact:* Expected impact relates to the changes that will occur for all key stakeholders in the transition systems. Will services improve? Communication? How will addressing the barrier change the current transition system? The expected impact should be tied directly to the barrier and needs statement. For example, the resource directory presented in the previous example should lead to staff having consistent information about programs and services available in the community. It may also lead to families having information about their options for services when their child makes a transition and/or information about other services and supports in the community that can help them meet their needs.

4. *Stakeholders/method of involvement:* All stakeholders who are either affected by the barrier or part of the system that helps create a barrier should be involved in some way in the development of the activity or practice designed to address the barrier. In other words, those who are part of the problem should also be part of the solution. The team should start by listing all stakeholder groups (e.g., teachers, families) or specific stakeholders if appropriate (e.g., school psychologist). Next, determine how these stakeholders will be involved in the design and implementation of the activity. This can include things such as serving as a member of a workgroup, participating in a focus group or interview, or serving as reviewers of a particular product or document.

5. *Resources and supports:* In Chapter 6, the team spent time identifying practices that already were in place within individual agencies. This information now can be used to help identify existing resources and supports that can be used when designing and implementing the practice. For example, one agency may already have developed a resource booklet that can be expanded to meet the team's needs. In addition, other resources (e.g., federal, state, regional, local) can be gathered and used to support the team.

6. *Evaluation of outcomes:* For each barrier addressed, the work plan includes an evaluation of the proposed outcome. This section is where specific ideas on the measure that will be used to gauge the effectiveness of the practices should be provided. The outcome measures should be linked with both the expected impacts and the needs statement.

The third section of the work plan includes the specific action steps that will outline how, when, and by whom the work will be done. These steps can be adapted or refined from the recommended steps provided in Chapters 7 and 8.

Team Summary of Transition Practices

Interagency structure	Timelines				Annual review dates				
	Proposed		Actual						
	Initiate	Complete	Initiate	Complete	1	2	3	4	5
1. Structure for operation and participation	Jun '05	Jul '05	Jun '05	Aug '05	Jun '06				
2. Authority of committee to make transition decisions—policies and procedures	Jun '05	Aug '05	Jun '05	Sep '05	Jun '06				
3. Authority of individuals to make agency decisions	Jun '05	Aug '05	Jun '05	Sep '05	Jun '06				
4. Complaint and problem-solving methods	Sep '05	Sep '05	Oct '05	Oct '05	Jun '06				
5. Authority of committee to make funding decisions—administration and services	Jun '05	Aug '05	Jun '05	Sep '05	Jun '06				
6. Meeting logistics (time, date, location)	Jun '05	Jul '05	Jun '05	Jul '05	Jun '06				
7. Committee leadership structure a. Leadership positions and responsibilities	Jun '05	Jul '05	Jun '05	Aug '05	Jun '06				
b. Rotation of leadership positions	Jun '05	Jul '05	Jun '05	Aug '05	Jun '06				
8. Team-building opportunities	Jun '05	Jul '05	Jun '05	Jul '05	Jun '06				
9. Effective meeting strategies a. Meeting structure (agenda)	Jul '05	Sep '05	Jul '05	Sep '05	Jul '06				
b. Brainstorming ground rules	Jul '05	Sep '05	Jul '05	Sep '05	Jul '06				
c. Discussion and meeting ground rules	Jul '05	Sep '05	Jul '05	Sep '05	Jul '06				
d. Recording techniques (minutes)	Jul '05	Sep '05	Jul '05	Sep '05	Jul '06				
10. Setting priorities	Jul '05	Sep '05	Jul '05	Sep '05	Jul '06				
11. Decision-making processes and ground rules	Jul '05	Sep '05	Jul '05	Sep '05	Jul '06				

Program practices: Activities	Timelines				Annual review dates				
	Proposed		Actual						
	Initiate	Complete	Initiate	Complete	1	2	3	4	5
1. Staff have key information about agencies and services available in the community.	Nov '05	Jun '06	Nov '05	Jun '06	Mar '07				
2. A single contact person for transition is identified from each agency.	Nov '05	Jun '06	Nov '05	Jun '06	Mar '07				
3. Broad-based transition activities and timelines are identified for (e.g., open house, Child Find).									
4. Processes are in place for child- and family-based transition meetings.									
5. Processes are in place for enrollment and referral.									
6. Processes are in place for screenings and evaluations.									
7. Processes are in place for follow-up on children in transition.									
8. Processes are in place to ensure that staff and family members are actively involved in transition system design.									
9. Staff roles and responsibilities for transition activities are outlined.									
10. There is continuity in curriculum and child expectations.	Jan '06	Jan '07	Jan '06						
11. Methods are in place to support staff-to-staff communication.									
12. Information about children making a transition is shared.	Jan '06	Jun '06	Jan '06	Jun '06	Jun '07				
13. Individual transition plans are developed for each child and family									
14. Children have opportunities to develop the entry-level skills they need to be successful in the receiving environment.	Jan '06	Jan '07	Jan '06						
15. Families are aware of the importance of transition planning and have the information they need to actively participate in transition planning with their child.									
16. Families participate as partners with staff in transition-planning activities.									
17. Families' needs related to transition are assessed and addressed.	Jun '06	Jun '07	Jun '06						
18. Families actively participate in gathering information about their child's growth and development.									
19. Families have information about additional resources and services to help them meet their specific child and family needs.	Jan '06	Jan '07	Jan '06						

Figure 10.4. Team summary of transition practices (sample).

TRACKING LONG-RANGE IMPLEMENTATION OF PRACTICES

One advantage to developing a community plan is that it helps keep all agencies on the same page when it comes to transition planning. The secret to a successful transition lies in continuity of the process between the sending and receiving agencies. Keeping track of the implementation of practices over time is also important. This provides a chronicled history of the work of the team, which is especially helpful as new team members join the team.

Keeping track of the practices and activities implemented by the team can occur using a blank, photocopiable version of Figure 10.4, which can be found on page 189 in the appendix. This form allows the team to document projected initiation and completion dates for each practice and then to record the actual initiation and completion dates. Keeping track of this information will help the team better gauge the amount of time needed to complete implementation. The form also allows the team to document annual reviews of each of the practices they have chosen to implement to determine whether they are still working or if refinement is needed. Additional initiation and completion dates can be entered if the team chooses to revisit a specific practice to make changes or additions.

SUMMARY

This chapter provides information, strategies, and forms that can be used to help the team organize the work proposed, plan the steps that need to be taken, and document the implementation of specific practices in the community. As many team members know, talk is easy; the hard part is getting the plan on paper and then following through with the plan.

Chapter 11

Evaluation

Evaluating and documenting our efforts to support high-quality transition practices for young children and their families provides an opportunity for us to reflect on our practices, consider new and revised approaches, and renew our commitment to maintain those practices that are effective in supporting the children and families we serve. Program evaluation often is defined as carefully collecting information about a program, or some aspect of it, in order to make necessary decisions about the program (McNamara, 1998). Although transition efforts typically cross programs, the program evaluation literature provides a helpful framework for planning evaluation efforts. As you think about evaluating your transition efforts, consider the standards that the Joint Committee on Standards for Educational Evaluation (1994) developed for designing evaluations. Within this design, three components are most critical for evaluating the transition activities in a community.

The first component is utility. The evaluation activities should be selected and implemented to ensure that the transition committee gets the information it needs to improve the community system of transition services, which is the overall goal of the transition process described in this book. In addition, the evaluation activities also should take into consideration the individual agency needs related to transition information. For example, for one agency it might be important to evaluate the degree to which they are meeting state or federal regulations; in another agency, the most critical factor might be that families receive the information they need to be involved with their child in the transition process.

The second component is feasibility. The process and procedures designed to gather information on the transition experiences of staff, families, and children should be realistic and sensitive enough to ensure that the data are meaningful to all involved. This includes using multiple and appropriate sources of data and measures of those experiences.

The third area is propriety. The evaluation should be conducted ethically and appropriately and with regard to the multiple stakeholders involved in the transition efforts within the community. More specifically, information gathered through the evaluation process must be shared with a variety of stakeholders, including an advisory group, staff, families, and the community at large so that critical decisions can be made about the program.

EVALUATING SPECIFIC TRANSITION ACTIVITIES AND PRACTICES

Integrating the processes of evaluation within the transition framework designed to support transition at the local level is essential. As local teams develop interagency transition plans and design community transition activities, the evaluation of those efforts should be integrated into initial planning. The action plan presented in Chapter 10 provides a mechanism for local teams to integrate evaluation into their plan. Many different types of evaluation strategies can be identified and applied to transition practices. However, the type of evaluation strategy used depends on the types of transition practices implemented locally. In other words, the transition plan and practices that are implemented at the community level depend on local needs. In turn, the evaluation strategies selected will reflect the actual transition practices selected for local use.

Planning for high-quality evaluation transition practices will lend credibility to transition efforts and provide accountability for resources directed at transition practices. Consider the following three examples:

- Most parents of children enrolled in the local early intervention agency report that their transition planning was effective, helpful, and facilitated their adjustment to preschool special education services.

- Early intervention and preschool staff members demonstrate high levels of knowledge of IDEA (Individuals with Disabilities Education Act) transition regulations on a post-training questionnaire.

- Local agencies report that the local interagency agreement provided a framework for revising transition policies and procedures within their respective organizations.

These examples reflect data from different stakeholders—families, staff, and administration—regarding the effectiveness of transition practices at different levels of the local system. They also suggest that specific transition practices were helpful in improving transition for children and families.

To integrate evaluation into the local transition plan, the transition team needs to be able to respond to the following questions relative to a particular transition activity:

1. What is the expected outcome of this activity?

2. Who will directly benefit from this activity (e.g., teachers, children and families, administrators)?

3. How will they benefit (e.g., increased knowledge, change in practice, rate of participation)?

4. What are the best ways to gather information about the change (e.g., surveys, interviews, observations)?

5. Who needs to receive and understand these outcomes (e.g., families, policy makers, local administrators)?

Answers to these questions will drive the selection and implementation of appropriate and effective evaluation activities. Consider the following evaluations.

Evaluation Scenario #1

In the Hobart County community, the interagency community group has implemented two primary strategies to facilitate communication among the agencies involved in early care and education services in their county. Evaluation activities were integrated into each of these transition activities:

On-line resource guide: An on-line community resource guide was developed to maintain updated contact and eligibility information for community agencies. A large nonprofit child care organization hosts the resource guide as part of its web site. The resource guide is updated as needed. Users of the resource guide can link to a comments form and provide feedback regarding the guide and its use. This process has led to several improvements in the resource guide, including the addition of mental health services and links to useful parent education web sites.

Staff training: Staff from Head Start, early intervention, public school, preschool, and child care were jointly trained in ways of engaging families in the transition process. The training began with a pretest to determine participant level of knowledge about this topic; a post-test on the material was given at the end of the training to document the results of the training.

Evaluation Scenario #2

In Metroville, the local interagency group has targeted the transition to kindergarten as its primary focus. Some of the transition activities designed for this community include family meetings and common assessment procedures across sites to facilitate transition.

Family meetings: Family meetings are being held in the spring at preschool sites in an effort to provide information to parents regarding how to prepare and support their children's transitions to the kindergarten environment. Evaluation has been integrated into the design of this activity in two ways: 1) Family attendance is being aggregated across activities in an effort to document parent participation; and 2) Participants are completing a survey evaluating the content of the sessions.

Common assessment procedures: Several large community preschool programs worked in collaboration with the local kindergarten to develop a coordinated child-assessment process that includes the adoption of a common curriculum-based assessment tool. Preschool programs initiate the use of the tool and gather ongoing data. These data are then shared with the kindergarten programs. The local kindergarten program then continues to use the tool to provide continuity for the child and family. The purpose of this transition activity to align preschool and kindergarten programs with the evaluation therefore includes multiple components. Initially, survey data were collected from both preschool and kindergarten teachers regarding both the effectiveness of the assessment tool as well as the process used to share information across programs and with families. These evaluation data were used to streamline the information-sharing process among preschool and kindergarten programs. A large-scale evaluation was designed in conjunction with a local university to determine if the implementation of a common tool improves child outcomes.

These examples highlight a few ways that local communities can use evaluation methods to improve their practice and document the impact of their efforts to improve the transition experiences of young children and families. They also emphasize the use of multiple methods (e.g., surveys, direct child assessment, comment forms) and multiple informants (e.g., teacher, child, administrator) to evaluate local transition activities.

EVALUATING THE COMMUNITY TRANSITION PROCESS

The second important component of evaluation is the ability of the team to determine the impact and progress of the team in implementing a transition system communitywide. This requires the team to evaluate on an annual basis its own progress in terms of the process, the structure they are using to support their joint activities, and the outcome of the collaboration. In other words, evaluate your plan and the impact of your plan.

The steps outlined in this book make up a basic planning cycle that involves eight basic steps (see Figure 11.1). This cycle recognizes that transition-system planning is an ongoing process, not a one-time event.

Assessment of needs—The process begins with a general assessment of what the community needs for effective transitions. This helps the team assess the current status of transition in the community and the processes that are currently in place across agencies to support transition planning. The assessment of needs (see Chapter 3) is completed as the team begins to identify its members and discuss its vision for what effective transition will look like at the end of the process.

Gathering information and identifying barriers—The team must spend a great deal of time gathering information on effective transition practices and identifying the specific barriers in the community that are preventing staff and families from realizing the vision of what transition should be. This process should guide the team toward specific action. Once barriers have been identified, the team must go through a process of how to gather specific information and how to address the most critical barriers (see Chapters 6 and 10).

Setting priorities—It is impossible for any team to address all of the barriers identified or to implement all of the strategies or practices that have been presented in this book. Therefore, the team must prioritize those barriers they consider most critical to overcome so that the planning process can begin in earnest.

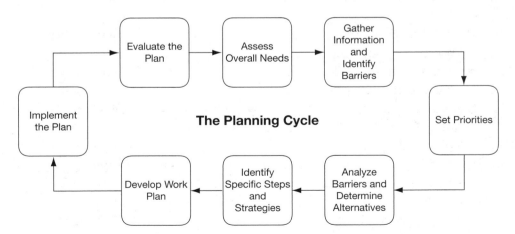

Figure 11.1. The planning cycle.

Analyzing barriers and determining alternatives—Chapters 7, 8, and 10 discussed information and supports for critically analyzing barriers and determining alternatives identified so that the team can understand and identify all of the alternatives they have available to overcome those barriers.

Identify strategies—Once the team has a common understanding of the barriers and problems, they can begin to brainstorm and identify strategies for addressing the barriers and choosing those practices that hold the most promise of success.

Developing a written work plan—The team works to develop a written work plan that outlines the steps to be taken.

Implement the practices—The most promising practices are put into place.

Evaluating the plan—The final step is for the team to evaluate the plan and the outcomes of the strategies implemented and make necessary adjustments and changes.

When evaluating the plan and the ability of the team to implement the plan, Figure 11.2 can provide a mechanism that the team can use on an annual basis to determine their progress and develop a new annual plan. This form provides a process for the team to determine the status of the interagency structure they have implemented to support their planning and the status of the use of standard practices in the community. A blank, photocopiable version of this form is provided on pages 190–192 in the appendix.

As local teams work together to reflect on the impact of their work on the community, the Community Transition System Impact Evaluation Survey (see

---

Community Transition System Impact Evaluation Survey

Date: _September 2006_

Please list the agencies involved in the transition process development in your community and indicate who was involved in completion of this form.

Agency: _Tri-State Early Intervention_ ☒ Involved in completion of this form

Agency: _Metroville Schools_ ☒ Involved in completion of this form

Agency: _Metroville Head Start_ ☒ Involved in completion of this form

Agency: _Young Kid Child Care_ ☐ Involved in completion of this form

Agency: _Metroville Health Department_ ☒ Involved in completion of this form

Agency: _Families Plus_ ☒ Involved in completion of this form

Agency: _____ ☐ Involved in completion of this form

Agency: _____ ☐ Involved in completion of this form

Agency: _____ ☐ Involved in completion of this form

Agency: _____ ☐ Involved in completion of this form

Agency: _____ ☐ Involved in completion of this form

Agency: _____ ☐ Involved in completion of this form

Was at least one family representative included on your transition team?   ☒ yes   ☐ no

Was that person included in the completion of this form?   ☒ yes   ☐ no

Figure 11.2. Community transition system impact evaluation survey (sample).

Section 1   *Directions*: Please circle your response.

Practice	Is this a **standard practice** in the community? Yes	No	If yes, do you have written guidelines (e.g.,) agreements, policies) that support this practice across agencies? Yes	No	If *yes* what is your perception of the impact of this practice on facilitating the transition process in your community for **program staff?** Much	Some	Little	None	If *yes* what is your perception of the impact of this practice on facilitating the transition process in your community for **families**? Much	Some	Little	None	If *yes* what is your perception of the impact of this practice on supporting positive transition outcomes in your community for **children**? Much	Some	Little	None
1. Staff have key information about agencies and services available in the community.	(Y)	N	(Y)	N	3	(2)	1	0	(3)	2	1	0	(3)	2	1	0
2. A single contact person for transition is identified from each agency.	(Y)	N	(Y)	N	(3)	2	1	0	3	(2)	1	0	3	(2)	1	0
3. Broad-based transition activities and timelines are identified (e.g., open house, Child Find).	Y	(N)	Y	N	3	2	1	0	3	2	1	0	3	2	1	0
4. Processes are in place for child- and family-based transition meetings.	Y	(N)	Y	N	3	2	1	0	3	2	1	0	3	2	1	0
5. Processes are in place for enrollment and referral.	Y	(N)	Y	N	3	2	1	0	3	2	1	0	3	2	1	0
6. Processes are in place for screenings and evaluations.	Y	(N)	Y	N	3	2	1	0	3	2	1	0	3	2	1	0
7. Processes are in place for follow-up on children in transition.	Y	(N)	Y	N	3	2	1	0	3	2	1	0	3	2	1	0
8. Processes are in place to ensure that staff and family members are actively involved in transition system design.	Y	(N)	Y	N	3	2	1	0	3	2	1	0	3	2	1	0
9. Staff roles and responsibilities for transition activities are outlined.	Y	(N)	Y	N	3	2	1	0	3	2	1	0	3	2	1	0
10. There is continuity in curriculum and child expectations.	Y	(N)	Y	N	3	2	1	0	3	2	1	0	3	2	1	0
11. Methods are in place to support staff-to-staff communication.	Y	(N)	Y	N	3	2	1	0	3	2	1	0	3	2	1	0
12. Information about children making a transition is shared.	(Y)	N	(Y)	N	(3)	2	1	0	3	(2)	1	0	(3)	2	1	0
13. Individual transition plans are developed for each child and family.	Y	(N)	Y	N	3	2	1	0	3	2	1	0	3	2	1	0
14. Children have opportunities to develop the entry-level skills they need to be successful in the receiving environment.	Y	(N)	Y	N	3	2	1	0	3	2	1	0	3	2	1	0

(continued)

Figure 11.2   *(continued)*

15. Families are aware of the importance of transition planning and have the information they need to actively participate in transition planning with their child.	Y	(N)	Y	N	3	2	1	0	3	2	1	0	3	2	1	0
16. Families participate as partners with staff in transition-planning activities.	Y	(N)	Y	N	3	2	1	0	3	2	1	0	3	2	1	0
17. Families' needs related to transition are assessed and addressed.	(Y)	N	(Y)	N	3	(2)	1	0	(3)	2	1	0	3	(2)	1	0
18. Families actively participate in gathering information about their child's growth and development.	Y	(N)	Y	N	3	2	1	0	3	2	1	0	3	2	1	0
19. Families have information about additional resources and services to help them meet their specific child and family needs.	(Y)	N	(Y)	N	(3)	2	1	0	(3)	2	1	0	(3)	2	1	0

SECTION 2

Directions: Choose up to three notable examples of contributions of the community transition process to facilitate the successful transition of young children in your community. These can be related to administration, staff, families, or children. For each selection, please describe the impact/outcome in your community and how the community planning process contributed to the impact/outcome.

Example #1	*Example #2*	*Example #3*
Description of barrier:	**Description of barrier:**	**Description of barrier:**
Personnel do not know about other agencies in the community so families do not have good information about their options		
Community process contribution:	**Community process contribution:**	**Community process contribution:**
A resource directory of community programs was developed to help staff link families with options in the community for services.		
Description of outcome/impact:	**Description of outcome/impact:**	**Description of outcome/impact:**
Staff are more consistent about sharing information about all options available for children and families. Cross-agency communication has increased.		

Please continue on another sheet if needed.

Figure 11.2) provides a mechanism by which teams can look across activities to examine the overall impact of the community system on the staff, the families, and the children. The results of the survey can provide information needed for the team to review the status of the central elements of an effective transition system (such as the identification of contact people and the establishment of common timelines) and assess their community progress relative to these practices. The entire group needs to complete the impact survey to ensure diverse perspectives on current practices. The survey also provides a means to identify key activities implemented within the community and describe their impact locally. This measure of impact can be augmented using the other evaluation measures described earlier in this chapter as they relate to specific transition practices. Thus, the impact survey can be used annually to document community progress towards more effective transition practices.

Evaluation of locally designed transition practices is an important element of community planning. As budgets tighten and policies change, local community teams can be accountable for their efforts by documenting their interagency activities and progressing toward more effective transition policies and practices for young children and families.

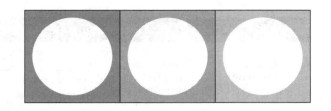

Appendix

Photocopiable Forms

Determining Community Relationships

Major stakeholder agencies	Transition-related activities	Current relationship			
		Communicate (exchange, respond)	Cooperate (comply, help)	Coordinate (organize, match)	Collaborate (join forces, pool)

Survey of Agencies and Programs	
Program/service	**Your community program/service name(s)**
Early intervention	
• Point of entry into system	
• Service coordination	
Public school	
• Preschool	
• Preschool special education	
• Even Start	
• Title I	
• Kindergarten/primary program	
Head Start	
Early Head Start	
Public health	
Mental health	
Social services	
Child care	
Specialized intervention programs	

Topic/time allotted	Action/process	Materials	Facilitator/discussant

Scope of Transitions Checklist

Transition points	Characteristics
☐ Hospital to home	☐ Children with specific disabilities (e.g., significant disabilities, visual impairments)
☐ Into infant/toddler services (Part C)	☐ Children with all identified disabilities
☐ Into preschool	☐ Children at risk for disabilities
☐ Into kindergarten	☐ Children at risk (e.g., poverty, abuse)
☐ Into primary school (e.g., first grade)	☐ All children
☐ Into intermediate school (e.g., fourth grade)	

Transition Team Participants

Agency name	Which staff positions need to be involved?

Given our scope, which transition points should be represented?	
How many family members should be included on the team?	
How will families be supported in their participation?	

Developing a Vision

Audience	Goals of effective transition planning
Young children	
Families	
Providers/teachers and other staff	
Administrators	

Determining Team Roles

Level of involvement	Key roles
Active participants (core team of 5–9 members):	
Resources (assist with information sharing and so forth as needed):	
Key stakeholders (those who need to be kept informed and from whom support is needed):	

Role	Term	Responsibility
Chairperson:		
Recorder:		
Gatekeeper:		
Timekeeper:		
Contact person:		
Other:		
Other:		
Other:		

Determining Team Responsibilities

Team Meeting Structure

Meeting component	Strategies or components
What general meeting guidelines will the group follow?	
How will the group address meeting logistics such as regular meeting time, dates, and locations?	
How will the leadership issues of the group be addressed, including leadership structure (e.g., facilitator, recorder), leadership election, rotation schedule, and role clarification?	
What are the group's rules for brainstorming?	
What are the group's rules for discussion?	
What group recording process will be used by the group?	
What opportunities will be provided for participants to get to know each other as individuals? (Building people-to-people relationships can have a major positive impact on interagency relationships.)	

Decision Making		
Decision-making technique	When the method will be used (Type of activity or action)	How the decision will be documented
Default		
Authority		
Majority		
Consensus		
Clique		
Other:		

Meeting Evaluation

You know you have had an effective meeting if you can agree with the following statements.

YES NO

☐   ☐   The ideas and talents of the council members have been well used.

☐   ☐   The time spent arriving at decisions was well used.

☐   ☐   The decisions made are correct or high in quality.

☐   ☐   The decisions made will be acted on by all individuals in the group.

☐   ☐   The decision-making ability of the group has been improved.

	Setting Priorities	
Method	To be used for	Process to be used
Dotting		
Voting		
Other		

Analyzing Interagency Communication

Agency: _____   Date completed: _____

1 = strongly agree, 2 = somewhat agree, 3 = somewhat disagree, 4 = strongly disagree

	Early intervention	Public school— preschool	Public school— school age	Head Start	Child care
We use primarily formal communication strategies (e.g., written) with this agency.	1 2 3 4	1 2 3 4	1 2 3 4	1 2 3 4	1 2 3 4
Contacting this agency is easy when I have questions or need to get in touch with them.	1 2 3 4	1 2 3 4	1 2 3 4	1 2 3 4	1 2 3 4
I am in contact with this agency on a regular basis as part of my work.	1 2 3 4	1 2 3 4	1 2 3 4	1 2 3 4	1 2 3 4
We have been able to work with this agency to solve common issues and address problems.	1 2 3 4	1 2 3 4	1 2 3 4	1 2 3 4	1 2 3 4
The staff members in this agency are responsive to my requests for information and assistance.	1 2 3 4	1 2 3 4	1 2 3 4	1 2 3 4	1 2 3 4
I am familiar with terminology used by this agency.	1 2 3 4	1 2 3 4	1 2 3 4	1 2 3 4	1 2 3 4
I am familiar with the specific transition activities regularly implemented by this agency.	1 2 3 4	1 2 3 4	1 2 3 4	1 2 3 4	1 2 3 4

Tools for Transition in Early Childhood: A Step-by-Step Guide for Agencies, Teachers, and Families
by Beth S. Rous & Rena A. Hallam. Copyright © 2007 by Paul H. Brookes Publishing Co., Inc. All rights reserved.

Assessing Status of Transition Activities

Use the following chart to assess the current status of transition practices and activities in individual agencies. Indicate the status of each practice by placing a ✓ in the appropriate column. If a practice is in place (partially or as a standard practice) indicate how that practice is supported in your agency. If you don't know, leave the column blank.

Transition practice or activity	Individual agency status				Practice is supported through		
	Not in place	Partially in place	Standard practice[1]	Don't know	Written procedure or agreement	Technical or written guidance	Nothing in writing
1. Staff have key information about agencies and services available in the community.							
2. A single contact person for transition is identified from each agency.							
3. Broad-based transition activities and timelines are identified (e.g., open house, Child Find).							
4. Processes are in place for child- and family-based transition meetings.							
5. Processes are in place for enrollment and referral.							
6. Processes are in place for screenings and evaluations.							
7. Processes are in place for follow-up on children in transition.							
8. Processes are in place to ensure that staff and family members are actively involved in transition system design.							

[1]Standard practice means that all staff in your agency or program regularly implement the activity or practice.

9. Staff roles and responsibilities for transition activities are outlined.							
10. There is continuity in curriculum and child expectations.							
11. Methods are in place to support staff-to-staff communication.							
12. Information about children making a transition is shared.							
13. Individual transition plans are developed for each child and family.							
14. Children have opportunities to develop the entry-level skills they need to be successful in the receiving environment.							
15. Families are aware of the importance of transition planning and have the information they need to actively participate in transition planning with their child.							
16. Families participate as partners with staff in transition-planning activities.							
17. Families' needs related to transition are assessed and addressed.							
18. Families actively participate in gathering information about their child's growth and development.							
19. Families have information about additional resources and services to help them meet their specific child and family needs.							

181

Child, Family, or Community Transition Plan

Date: _____ Community ☐ Program ☐ Family ☐ Child ☐

Family/child's name:_____

Child's date of birth:_____

Goal 1:_____

Indicator 1:_____

Indicator 2:_____

Indicator 3:_____

Steps/activities to support transition	Lead team member and others who need to be involved	Timeline	
		Date proposed	Date achieved

Barriers to transition	Priority barriers based on dotting approach

Linking Barriers to Transition Practices

Instructions: Using the list of barriers identified by the team, match barriers to those activities or practices that could help address the barriers. More than one barrier may be addressed through an activity, and some barriers can be addressed through multiple activities.

Transition practice or activity	Specific barriers addressed		
1. Staff have key information about agencies and services available in the community.			
2. A single contact person for transition is identified from each agency.			
3. Broad-based transition activities and timelines are identified (e.g., open house, Child Find).			
4. Processes are in place for child- and family-based transition meetings.			
5. Processes are in place for enrollment and referral.			
6. Processes are in place for screenings and evaluations.			
7. Processes are in place for follow-up on children in transition.			
8. Processes are in place to ensure that staff and family members are actively involved in transition system design.			
9. Staff roles and responsibilities for transition activities are outlined.			

184

10. There is continuity in curriculum and child expectations.									
11. Methods are in place to support staff-to-staff communication.									
12. Information about children making a transition is shared.									
13. Individual transition plans are developed for each child and family.									
14. Children have opportunities to develop the entry-level skills they need to be successful in the receiving environment.									
15. Families are aware of the importance of transition planning and have the information they need to actively participate in transition planning with their child.									
16. Families participate as partners with staff in transition-planning activities.									
17. Families' needs related to transition are assessed and addressed.									
18. Families actively participate in gathering information about their child's growth and development.									
19. Families have information about additional resources and services to help them meet their specific child and family needs.									

Community Transition Team Work Plan

Community: _____   Date: _____

Team members:

1.   5.

2.   6.

3.   7.

4.   8.

                                 .

Transition definition:

Transition points addressed:

Community vision statement:

Needs statement Statement of barriers to overcome				
Expected outcomes Products, events, and so forth that will be in place in response to the barrier				
Expected impact Change brought about as result of outcomes				
Stakeholders/method of involvement (e.g., surveys, focus group interviews, advisory committees)				
Resources and supports Resources that can be tapped for assistance				
Evaluation of outcomes Methods used to determine that expected outcomes have been achieved				

(continued)

(continued)

Action Plan

Outcome/objective: _____

Steps/activities needed for implementation	Timelines	Person responsible

Team Summary of Transition Practices

Interagency structure	Timelines				Annual review dates				
	Proposed		Actual		1	2	3	4	5
	Initiate	Complete	Initiate	Complete					
1. Structure for operation and participation									
2. Authority of committee to make transition decisions—policies and procedures									
3. Authority of individuals to make agency decisions									
4. Complaint and problem-solving methods									
5. Authority of committee to make funding decisions—administration and services									
6. Meeting logistics (time, date, location)									
7. Committee leadership structure a. Leadership positions and responsibilities									
b. Rotation of leadership positions									
8. Team-building opportunities									
9. Effective meeting strategies a. Meeting structure (agenda)									
b. Brainstorming ground rules									
c. Discussion and meeting ground rules									
d. Recording techniques (minutes)									
10. Setting priorities									
11. Decision-making processes and ground rules									

Program practices: Activities	Timelines				Annual review dates				
	Proposed		Actual		1	2	3	4	5
	Initiate	Complete	Initiate	Complete					
1. Staff have key information about agencies and services available in the community.									
2. A single contact person for transition is identified from each agency.									
3. Broad-based transition activities and timelines are identified for (e.g., open house, Child Find).									
4. Processes are in place for child- and family-based transition meetings.									
5. Processes are in place for enrollment and referral.									
6. Processes are in place for screenings and evaluations.									
7. Processes are in place for follow-up on children in transition.									
8. Processes are in place to ensure that staff and family members are actively involved in transition system design.									
9. Staff roles and responsibilities for transition activities are outlined.									
10. There is continuity in curriculum and child expectations.									
11. Methods are in place to support staff-to-staff communication.									
12. Information about children making a transition is shared.									
13. Individual transition plans are developed for each child and family									
14. Children have opportunities to develop the entry-level skills they need to be successful in the receiving environment.									
15. Families are aware of the importance of transition planning and have the information they need to actively participate in transition planning with their child.									
16. Families participate as partners with staff in transition-planning activities.									
17. Families' needs related to transition are assessed and addressed.									
18. Families actively participate in gathering information about their child's growth and development.									
19. Families have information about additional resources and services to help them meet their specific child and family needs.									

(continued)

Community Transition System Impact Evaluation Survey

Date:_____

Please list the agencies involved in the transition process development in your community and indicate who was involved in completion of this form.

Agency: _____ ☐ Involved in completion of this form

Agency: _____ ☐ Involved in completion of this form

Agency: _____ ☐ Involved in completion of this form

Agency: _____ ☐ Involved in completion of this form

Agency: _____ ☐ Involved in completion of this form

Agency: _____ ☐ Involved in completion of this form

Agency: _____ ☐ Involved in completion of this form

Agency: _____ ☐ Involved in completion of this form

Agency: _____ ☐ Involved in completion of this form

Agency: _____ ☐ Involved in completion of this form

Agency: _____ ☐ Involved in completion of this form

Agency: _____ ☐ Involved in completion of this form

Was at least one family representative included on your transition team? ☐ yes ☐ no

Were they included in the completion of this form? ☐ yes ☐ no

Section 1   *Directions*: Please circle your response.

Practice	Is this a **standard practice** in the community?		If yes, do you have written guidelines (e.g.,) agreements, policies) that support this practice across agencies?		If *yes* what is your perception of the impact of this practice on facilitating the transition process in your community for **program staff?**				If *yes* what is your perception of the impact of this practice on facilitating the transition process in your community for **families**?				If *yes* what is your perception of the impact of this practice on supporting positive transition outcomes in your community for **children**?			
	Yes	No	Yes	No	Much	Some	Little	None	Much	Some	Little	None	Much	Some	Little	None
1. Staff have key information about agencies and services available in the community.	Y	N	Y	N	3	2	1	0	3	2	1	0	3	2	1	0
2. A single contact person for transition is identified from each agency.	Y	N	Y	N	3	2	1	0	3	2	1	0	3	2	1	0
3. Broad-based transition activities and timelines are identified (e.g., open house, Child Find).	Y	N	Y	N	3	2	1	0	3	2	1	0	3	2	1	0
4. Processes are in place for child- and family-based transition meetings.	Y	N	Y	N	3	2	1	0	3	2	1	0	3	2	1	0
5. Processes are in place for enrollment and referral.	Y	N	Y	N	3	2	1	0	3	2	1	0	3	2	1	0
6. Processes are in place for screenings and evaluations.	Y	N	Y	N	3	2	1	0	3	2	1	0	3	2	1	0
7. Processes are in place for follow-up on children in transition.	Y	N	Y	N	3	2	1	0	3	2	1	0	3	2	1	0

8. Processes are in place to ensure that staff and family members are actively involved in transition system design.	Y	N	Y	N	3	2	1	0	3	2	1	0	3	2	1	0
9. Staff roles and responsibilities for transition activities are outlined.	Y	N	Y	N	3	2	1	0	3	2	1	0	3	2	1	0
10. There is continuity in curriculum and child expectations.	Y	N	Y	N	3	2	1	0	3	2	1	0	3	2	1	0
11. Methods are in place to support staff-to-staff communication.	Y	N	Y	N	3	2	1	0	3	2	1	0	3	2	1	0
12. Information about children making a transition is shared.	Y	N	Y	N	3	2	1	0	3	2	1	0	3	2	1	0
13. Individual transition plans are developed for each child and family.	Y	N	Y	N	3	2	1	0	3	2	1	0	3	2	1	0
14. Children have opportunities to develop the entry-level skills they need to be successful in the receiving environment.	Y	N	Y	N	3	2	1	0	3	2	1	0	3	2	1	0
15. Families are aware of the importance of transition planning and have the information they need to actively participate in transition planning with their child.	Y	N	Y	N	3	2	1	0	3	2	1	0	3	2	1	0
16. Families participate as partners with staff in transition-planning activities.	Y	N	Y	N	3	2	1	0	3	2	1	0	3	2	1	0
17. Families' needs related to transition are assessed and addressed.	Y	N	Y	N	3	2	1	0	3	2	1	0	3	2	1	0
18. Families actively participate in gathering information about their child's growth and development.	Y	N	Y	N	3	2	1	0	3	2	1	0	3	2	1	0
19. Families have information about additional resources and services to help them meet their specific child and family needs.	Y	N	Y	N	3	2	1	0	3	2	1	0	3	2	1	0

(continued)

(continued)

SECTION 2

Directions: Choose up to three notable examples of contributions of the community transition process to facilitate the successful transition of young children in your community. These can be related to administration, staff, families, or children. For each selection, please describe the impact/outcome in your community and how the community planning process contributed to the impact/outcome.

Example #1	*Example #2*	*Example #3*
Description of barrier:	**Description of barrier:**	**Description of barrier:**

_____

_____

_____

_____

_____

Community process contribution: **Community process contribution:**   **Community process contribution:**

_____

_____

_____

_____

_____

Description of outcome/impact: **Description of outcome/impact:**   **Description of outcome/impact:**

_____

_____

_____

_____

_____

Please continue on another sheet if needed.

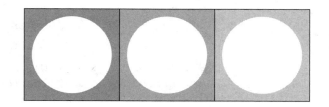

References

Amason, A.C., Thompson, K.R., Hochwarter, W.A., & Harrison, A.W. (1995). Conflict: An important dimension in successful management teams. *Organizational Dynamics, 24*(2), 20–35.

Barnett, W.S., Hustedt, J.T., Robin, K.B., & Schulman, K.L. (2004). *The state of preschool: 2004 state preschool yearbook.* New Brunswick, NJ: National Institute for Early Education Research.

Bellah, R., Madsen, R., Sullivan, W., Swidler, A., & Tipton, S. (1985). *Habits of the heart: Individualism and commitment in American life:* New York: Harper and Row.

Berstene, T. (2004). The inexorable link between conflict and change. *Journal for Quality & Participation, 27*(2), 5–9.

Blank, H., Schulman, K., & Ewen, D. (1999). *Key facts: Essential information about child care, early education, and school-age care.* Washington, DC: Children's Defense Fund.

Bredekamp, S., & Copple, C. (1997). *Developmentally appropriate practice in early childhood programs* (Rev. ed.). Washington, DC: National Association for the Education of Young Children.

Breznay, S. (2001). Liaison teams: A strategy for building interagency collaboration in caring for children with serious emotional disturbances and their families. *Issues in Interdisciplinary Care, 3*(2), 101–105.

Bronfenbrenner, U. (1986). Ecology of the family as a context for human development: Research perspectives. *Developmental Psychology, 22*(6), 723–742.

Bronfenbrenner, U., & Morris, P.A. (1998). The ecology of developmental processes. In R.S. Lerner (Ed.), *Handbook of child psychology* (5th ed., Vol. 1, pp. 993–1028). New York: John Wiley and Sons.

Byrd, R., Stephens, P., Dyk, L., Perry, E., & Rous, B. (1991). *Sequenced transition to education in the public schools: Project STEPS replication manual.* (2nd ed.). Lexington: University of Kentucky.

Chandler, L.K. (1993). Steps in preparing for transition: Preschool to kindergarten. *Teaching Exceptional Children, 25*(4), 52–55.

Children's Defense Fund. (2003). *Quality child care helps parents work and children learn.* Retrieved May 23, 2003, from http://www.childrensdefense.org/earlychildhood/childcare

Conn-Powers, M.C., Ross-Allen, J., & Holburn, S. (1990). Transition of young children into the elementary education mainstream. *Topics in Early Childhood Special Education, 9*(4), 91–105.

Diamond, K.E., Reagan, A.J., & Bandyk, J.E. (2000). Parents' conceptions of kindergarten readiness: Relationships with race, ethnicity, and development. *Journal of Educational Research, 94*(2), 93–100.

Dodge, D.T., Colker, L.J., Heroman, C., & Bickart, T.S. (2002). *The Creative Curriculum* (4th ed.). Washington, DC: Teaching Strategies.

Dunst, C.J., Hamby, D., Trivette, C.M., Raab, M., & Bruder, M.B. (2000). Everyday family and community life and children's naturally occurring learning opportunities. *Journal of Early Intervention, 23*(3), 151–164.

Education of the Handicapped Act Amendments of 1986, PL 99-457, 20 U.S.C. §§ 1400 *et seq.*

Edwards, G. (1980). *Implementing public policy.* Washington, DC: Congressional Quarterly Press.

Entwisle, D.R., & Alexander, K.L. (1998). Facilitating the transition to first grade: The nature of transition and research on factors affecting it. *Elementary School Journal, 98*(4), 351–364.

Family Educational Rights and Privacy Act (FERPA) of 1974, PL 93-380, 34 C.F.R. Part 99.

Fawcett, S. (2003). Building capacity for participatory evaluation within community initiatives. *Journal of Prevention & Intervention in the Community, 26*(2), 21–36.

Flaspohler, P. (2003). Promoting program success and fulfilling accountability requirements in a statewide community-based initiative: Challenges, progress, and lessons learned. *Journal of Prevention & Intervention in the Community, 26*(2), 37–52.

Fowler, S.A., Chandler, L.K., Johnson, T.E., & Stella, E. (1988). Individualizing family involvement in school transitions: Gathering information and choosing the next program. *Journal of the Division for Early Childhood, 12*(3), 208–216.

Francis, D., & Young, D. (1992). *Improving work groups: A practical manual for team building.* San Diego, CA: Pfeiffer & Company.

Fraser, B.J., & Fisher, D.L. (1986). Using short forms of classroom climate instruments to assess and improve classroom psychosocial environment. *Journal of Research in Science Teaching, 23,* 387–413.

Gallagher, J.J. (1994). Personal patterns of underachievement. *Journal for the Education of the Gifted, 14,* 221–233.

Gamel-McCormick, M., & Rous, B. (2000). *Delaware: Transition study report.* Newark: University of Delaware.

Glicksman, K., & Hills, T. (1981). *Easing the child's transition between home, child care center and school: A guide for early childhood educators.* Trenton: New Jersey State Department of Education.

Hadden, S., Fowler, S., Fink, D., & Wischnowski, M. (1995). *Writing an interagency agreement on transition: A practical guide. Family and child transitions into least restrictive education (FACTS/LRE).* University of Illinois at Urbana-Champaign.

Hanline, M.F. (1988). Making the transition to preschool: Identification of parent needs. *Journal of the Division for Early Childhood, 12*(2), 98–107.

Hanline, M.F. (1993). Facilitating integrated preschool service delivery transitions for children, families, and professionals. In C.A. Peck, S.L. Odom, & D.D. Bricker (Eds.), *Integrating young children with disabilities into community programs: Ecological perspectives on research and implementation* (pp. 133–146). Baltimore: Paul H. Brookes Publishing Co.

Harbin, G.L., Bruder, M.B., Adams, C., Mazzarella, C., Whitbread, K., Gabbard, G., et al. (2004). Early intervention service coordination policies: National policy infra-structure. *Topics in Early Childhood Special Education, 24,* 89–97.

Harbin, G.L., McWilliam, R.A., & Gallagher, J.J. (2000). Services for young children with disabilities and their families. In J.P. Shonkoff & J.P Meisels (Eds.), *Handbook of early childhood intervention.* New York: Cambridge University Press.

Harbin, G., Rous, B., & McLean, M. (2005). Issues in designing state accountability systems. *Journal of Early Intervention, 27*(3).

Harbin, G.L., & Salisbury, C. (2000). Policies, administration, and systems change. In S. Sandall, M.E. McLean, & B.J. Smith (Eds.), *DEC recommended practices in early intervention/early childhood special education* (pp. 65–69). Longmont, CO: Sopris West.

Harbin, G.L., McWilliam, R.A., Shaw, D., Buka, S.L., Sideris, J., & Kochaek, T.T., et al. (1998). *Implementing federal policy for young children with disabilities: How are we doing?* Chapel Hill, NC: FPG Child Development Center, University of North Carolina. (ERIC Document Reproduction Service No. ED417527)

Health Insurance Portability and Accountability Act (HIPAA) of 1996, PL 104-191, 42 U.S.C. §§ 201 *et seq.*

Hemmeter, M.L., & Rous, B. (1997). *Teachers' expectations of children's transition into kindergarten or ungraded primary programs: A national survey.* Unpublished manuscript.

Hollenbeck, J.R., Ilgen, D.R., LePine, J.A., Colquitt, J.A., & Hedlund, J. (1998). Extending the multilevel theory of team decision making: Effects of feedback and experience in hierarchical teams. *Academy of Management Journal, 41*(3), 269–282.

Hoover-Dempsey, K.V., & Sandler, H.M. (1997). Why do parents become involved in their children's education? *Review of Educational Research, 67*(1), 3–42.

Hopen, D. (2004). Conflict: The key to innovation. *Journal for Quality & Participation, 27*(2), 3.

Howell, E.N. (1994). *Supported transition into kindergarten for preschool students with special needs.* Unpublished master's thesis, Grand Valley State University, Allendale, MI.

Individuals with Disabilities Education Act (IDEA) of 1990, PL 101-476, 20 U.S.C. §§ 1400 *et seq.*

Individuals with Disabilities Education Improvement Act of 2004, PL 108-446, 20 U.S.C. §§ 1400 *et seq.*

Jang, M., & Mangione, P.L. (1994). *Transition program practices: Improving linkages between early childhood education and early elementary school.* Washington, DC: U.S. Department of Education.

Johnson, D.W. (1980). Group processes: Influences on student-student interaction and school outcomes. In J. McMillan (Ed.), *Social psychology of school learning.* New York: Academic Press.

Johnson, D.W., & Johnson, R. (1975). *Learning together and alone: Cooperation, competition and individualization.* Englewood Cliffs, NJ: Prentice Hall.

Johnson, L., Gallagher, R., Cook, M., & Wong, P. (1995). Critical skills for kindergarten: Perceptions from kindergarten teachers. *Journal of Early Intervention, 19*(4), 315–327.

Joint Committee on Standards for Educational Evaluation. (1994). *The program evalua-*

tion standards. Thousand Oaks, CA: Sage Publications.

Kagan, S.L. (1992). The strategic importance of linkages and the transition between early childhood programs and early elementary school. In *Sticking together: Strengthening linkages and the transition between early childhood education and early elementary school (Summary of a National Policy Forum)*. Washington, DC: U.S. Department of Education.

Kakvoulis, A. (1994). Continuity in early childhood education: Transition from preschool to school. *International Journal of Early Years Education, 2*(1), 41–51.

Karr-Jelinek, C. (1994). *Transition to kindergarten: Parents and teachers working together.* Brazil, IN: ERIC Clearinghouse for Elementary and Early Childhood Education. (ERIC Document Reproduction Service No. ED371858)

Katims, D.S., & Pierce, P.L. (1995). Literacy-rich environments and the transition of young children with special needs. *Topics in Early Childhood Special Education, 15*(2), 219–234.

Kochanek, T.T., Costa, C.H., McGinn, J., & Cummins, C. (1997). *Maternal satisfaction with infant/toddler and preschool services.* Providence: Rhode Island College, School of Education, Early Childhood Research Institute on Service Utilization.

Love, J.M., Logue, M., Trudeau, J., & Thayer, K. (1992). *Transitions to kindergarten in American schools: Final report of the national transition study.* Portsmouth, NH: RMC Research Corp.

MacAulay, D.J. (1990). Classroom environment: A literature review. *Educational Psychology, 10*(3), 239–254.

Magnuson, K.A., Meyers, M.K., & Ruhm, C.J. (2004). Inequality in preschool education and school readiness. *American Educational Research Journal, 41*, 115–157.

Mangione, P.L., & Speth, T. (1998). The transition to elementary school: A framework for creating early childhood continuity through home, school, and community partnership. *Elementary School Journal, 98*(4), 381–397.

McNamara, C. (1998). *Basic guide to program evaluation.* Retrieved May 10, 2004, from http://www.mapnp.org/library

Meier, D., & Schafran, A. (1999). Strengthening the preschool-to-kindergarten transition: A community collaborates. *Young Children, 54*(3), 40–46.

Moles, O.C. (1993). Collaboration between schools and disadvantaged parents: Obstacles and openings. In N. Chavkin (Ed.), *Families and schools in a pluralistic society.* Albany: State University of New York Press.

National Center for Early Development and Learning. (December, 1999). *An approach to enhance kindergarten transition. NCEDL Spotlight #17.* Chapel Hill: University of North Carolina at Chapel Hill.

National Institute of Child Health and Human Development. (2002). Early child care and children's development prior to school entry: Results from the NICHD Study of Early Child Care. *American Educational Research Journal, 39*, 133–164.

No Child Left Behind Act of 2001, PL 107-110, 115 Stat. 1425, 20 U.S.C. §§ 6301 *et seq.*

Olsen, D.A. (1999). *Universal preschool is no golden ticket: Why government should not enter the preschool business* (Policy Analysis No. 333). Washington, DC: Cato Institute.

Peisner-Feinberg, E.S., Burchinal, M.R., Clifford, R.M., Yazejian, N., Culkin, M.L., Zelazo, J., et al. (2000). *The children of the cost, quality, and outcomes study go to school: Technical report.* Chapel Hill, NC: University of North Carolina at Chapel Hill, FPG Child Development Institute.

Pianta, R.C., & Cox, M.J. (1999). The changing nature of the transition to school: Trends for the next decade. In R.C. Pianta & M.J. Cox (Eds.), *The Transition to kinder-*

garten (pp. 363–379). Baltimore: Paul H. Brookes Publishing Co.

Pianta, R.C., Cox, M.J., Taylor, L., & Early, D. (1999). Kindergarten teachers' practices related to the transition to school: Results of a national survey. *Elementary School Journal, 100*(1), 71–86.

Pianta, R.C., & Kraft-Sayre, M. (2003). *Successful kindergarten transition: Your guide to connecting children, families, & schools.* Baltimore: Paul H. Brookes Publishing Co.

Pianta, R.C., Rimm-Kaufman, S.E., & Cox, M.J. (1999). Introduction: An ecological approach to kindergarten transition. In R.C. Pianta & M.J. Cox (Eds.), *The Transition to kindergarten* (pp. 3–12). Baltimore: Paul H. Brookes Publishing Co.

Pianta, R., & Walsh, D. (1996). *High-risk children in schools: Constructing sustaining relationships.* New York: Routledge.

Ramey, C.T., & Ramey, S.L. (2004). Early learning and school readiness: Can early intervention make a difference? *Merrill-Palmer Quarterly, 50,* 471–491.

Ramey, S.L., & Ramey, T. (1994). The transition to school: Why the first few years matter for a lifetime. *Phi Delta Kappan, 76*(3), 194–198.

Ramey, S.L., & Ramey T. (1998). The transition to school: Opportunities and challenges for children, families, educators, and communities. *Elementary School Journal, 98*(4), 293–295.

Repetto, J.B., & Correa, V.I. (1996). Expanding views on transition. *Exceptional Children, 62*(6), 551–563.

Rice, M.L., & O'Brien, M. (1990). Transitions: Times of change and accommodation. *Topics in Early Childhood Special Education, 9*(4), 1–14.

Rimm-Kaufmann, S.E., & Pianta, R.C. (1999). Patterns of family-school contact in preschool and kindergarten. *School Psychology Review, 28*(3), 426–438.

Rosenkoetter, S.E., Hains, A.H., & Fowler, S.A. (1994). *Bridging early services for children with special needs and their families: A practical guide for transition planning.* Baltimore: Paul H. Brookes Publishing Co.

Rosenkoetter, S.E., Whaley, K., Hains, A.H., & Pierce, L. (2001). The evolution of transition policy for young children with special needs and their families: Past, present and future. *Topics in Early Childhood Special Education, 1,* 3–15.

Rous, B. (2001). An evaluation of the special needs referral process. *Early Childhood Research Quarterly, 14,* 485–487.

Rous, B., & Hallam, R. (2002). Easing the transition to kindergarten: Assessment of social, behavioral and functional skills in young children with disabilities. In M. Ostrosky & E. Horn (Eds.), *Assessment: Gathering meaningful data* (pp. 97–110). Longmont, CO: Sopris West.

Rous, B., Hemmeter, M.L., & Schuster, J. (1994). Sequenced transition to education in the public schools: A systems approach to transition planning. *Topics in Early Childhood Special Education, 14,* 374–393.

Rous, B., Hemmeter, M.L., & Schuster, J. (1999). Evaluating the impact of the STEPS model on development of community-wide transition systems. *Journal of Early Intervention, 22*(1), 38–50.

Rous, B., McCormick, K., & Hallam, R. (2006). *Transition to preschool: Findings from a national survey.* Manuscript in preparation. Lexington: University of Kentucky National Early Childhood Transition Center.

Rule, S., Fiechtl, B., & Innocenti, M. (1990). Preparation for transition to mainstreamed post-preschool environments: Development of a survival skills curriculum. *Topics in Early Childhood Special Education, 9*(4), 78–90.

Sabatier, P., & Mazmanian, D. (1979). The conditions of effective implementation: A guide to accomplishing policy objectives. *Policy Analysis, 5*(4), 481–504.

Salisbury, C., Palombaro, M., & Hollowood, T. (1993). On the nature and change of inclusive schools. *Journal of the Association for Persons with Severe Handicaps, 18*(2), 75–84.

Schulting, A.B., Malone, P.S., & Dodge, K.A. (2005). The effects of school-based kindergarten transition policies on child academic outcomes. *Developmental Psychology, 41*(6), 860–871.

Swan, W.W., & Morgan, J.L. (1993). *Collaborating for comprehensive services for young children and their families: The local interagency coordinating council.* Baltimore: Paul H. Brookes Publishing Co.

Thurman, S.K. (1997). Systems, ecologies, and the context of early intervention. In S.K. Thurman, J.R. Cornwell, & S.R. Gottwald (Eds.), *Contexts of early intervention: Systems and settings* (pp. 3–17). Baltimore: Paul H. Brookes Publishing Co.

Tuckman, B. (1965). Developmental sequence in small groups. *Psychological Bulletin, 63,* 384–399.

Turnbull, R., & Turnbull, A. (1997). The constitutional and programmatic grounding of IDEA. *Journal for the Association for Persons with Severe Handicaps, 22*(2), 83–85.

U.S. Census Bureau. (2004). America Community Survey. Washington, DC: Author. Available at http://www.census.gov

U.S. Department of Education. (1988). *Tenth annual report to Congress on the implementation of the Education of the Handicapped Act.* Washington, DC: Office of Special Education Programs.

U.S. Department of Education. (2003). *Twenty-fifth annual report to Congress on the implementation of the Individuals with Disabilities Education Act, Vol. 1.* Washington, DC: Office of Special Education Programs.

U.S. Department of Education. (2004). *Twenty-sixth annual report to Congress on the implementation of the Individuals with Disabilities Education Act.* Washington, DC: Office of Special Education Programs.

U.S. Department of Health & Human Services. (2001, January). *Building their futures: How Early Head Start programs are enhancing the lives of infants and toddlers in low-income families.* Washington, DC: The Commissioner's Office of Research and Evaluation and the Head Start Bureau.

U.S. Department of Health & Human Services, (2002). *Making a difference in the lives of infants and toddlers and their families: The impacts of early head start.* Washington, DC: The Commissioner's Office of Research and Evaluation and the Head Start Bureau.

Van Horn, C., & Van Meter, D. (1977). The implementation of intergovernmental policy. In S. Nagel (Ed.), *Policy studies review annual* (Vol. 1). Beverly Hills, CA: Sage Publications.

Wheeler, W.P., Reetz, L.J., & Wheeler, J.J. (1993). Facilitating effective transition in early intervention services: Parent involvement. *Rural Special Education Quarterly, 12*(1), 55–60.

Williams, W. (1971). *Social policy research and analysis: The experience of federal social agencies.* New York: American Elsevier.

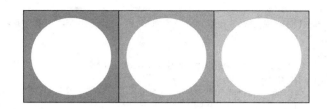

Index

Page references followed by *f* indicate figures; those followed by *t* indicate tables.